STRAVINSKY

PETRUSHKA

An Authoritative Score of the Original Version

Backgrounds · Analysis

Essays, Views, and Comments

NORTON CRITICAL SCORES

BACH **CANTATA NO. 4**
edited by Gerhard Herz

BACH **CANTATA NO. 140**
edited by Gerhard Herz

BEETHOVEN **SYMPHONY NO. 5 IN C MINOR**
edited by Elliot Forbes

BERLIOZ **FANTASTIC SYMPHONY**
edited by Edward T. Cone

CHOPIN **PRELUDES, OPUS 28**
edited by Thomas Higgins

DEBUSSY **PRELUDE TO "THE AFTERNOON OF A FAUN"**
edited by William W. Austin

MOZART **PIANO CONCERTO IN C MAJOR, K. 503**
edited by Joseph Kerman

MOZART **SYMPHONY IN G MINOR, K. 550**
edited by Nathan Broder

PALESTRINA **POPE MARCELLUS MASS**
edited by Lewis Lockwood

PURCELL **DIDO AND AENEAS**
edited by Curtis Price

SCHUBERT **SYMPHONY IN B MINOR ("UNFINISHED")**
edited by Martin Chusid

SCHUMANN **DICHTERLIEBE**
edited by Arthur Komar

STRAVINSKY **PETRUSHKA**
edited by Charles Hamm

WAGNER **PRELUDE AND TRANSFIGURATION**
from *TRISTAN AND ISOLDE*
edited by Robert Bailey

Igor Stravinsky

PETRUSHKA

An Authoritative Score of
the Original Version
Backgrounds · Analysis
Essays, Views, and Comments

Edited by

CHARLES HAMM

DARTMOUTH COLLEGE

W · W · NORTON & COMPANY

New York · London

W. W. Norton & Company, Inc., 500 Fifth Avenue, New York, N.Y. 10110

Library of Congress Catalog Card No. 67-17012

PRINTED IN THE UNITED STATES OF AMERICA

7 8 9 0

ISBN 0-393-09770-8

Contents

THE GENESIS
OF PETRUSHKA

The Genesis of Petrushka

Petrushka [1] is most often encountered today in the concert hall, or heard on the phonograph or radio, but it was conceived as a ballet and for many years known, enjoyed, and discussed as a stage work. Thus, an account of its early history must deal with it origin and adventures as a ballet, and it is impossible to separate this story from at least a partial account of the famous Ballets Russes troupe of Serge Diaghilev.

Diaghilev was a genius of sorts, talented in many things but perhaps ultimately most talented in recognizing genius in others and persuading them to work with him and with the other geniuses he assembled. After an early career in art and music in Russia, he came to Paris in 1906 to organize an exhibition of Russian painting in the Salon d'Automne, where he filled twelve rooms with Russian portraits from various historical periods. Paris was experiencing a cultural and intellectual explosion at this time and was becoming a rallying ground for artists from all over the world. A burgeoning internationalism was replacing the often homely nationalism of the previous century, and artists were turning for ideas to the Near East, the Orient, Africa, and even America. The Russian paintings created a stir, with their glowing colors and exotic vitality, and Diaghilev followed with a series of concerts of Russian music the next year, offering five programs of pieces by Rimsky-Korsakov, Glazunov, Rachmaninov, and Scriabin.

In 1908 he brought *Boris Godunov* to Paris, with Chaliapin in the title role, and the following year he organized a company to give programs of opera and ballet in the spring. Such ballets as the *Polovtsian Dances* from *Prince Igor, Les Sylphides,* and *Le Pavillon d'Armide* made

1. The Russian title of the ballet has been transliterated in various ways; the spelling *Petrushka* is used here except in passages quoted from other sources.

a great sensation because of the vivid settings by such artists as Benois and Bakst, the imaginative choreography of young Michel Fokine, the lively music by assorted Russian composers, and above all because of the breathtaking dancing by Pavlova, Fokine, Karsavina, and a young man named Nijinsky who had just completed his schooling.

A sensation of the second season of the Ballets Russes was a new ballet with music by a young, almost unknown Russian composer named Igor Stravinsky. He had first come to Diaghilev's attention when two of his compositions, *Scherzo fantastique* and *Fireworks,* were played at the Siloti concerts, and Diaghilev had asked him to do part of the orchestration of Chopin's music for the ballet *Les Sylphides.* Diaghilev, who wanted to introduce several completely new ballets for the 1910 season, had asked Liadov to compose music to a scenario based on the Russian fairy tale of the Firebird, but Liadov was a notoriously slow worker and was unable to promise that he would have his score ready in time; so Diaghilev, with the unerring instinct that so often enabled him to recognize great talent in young and relatively untested artists, without hesitation commissioned Stravinsky to do the score. *The Firebird,* with scenario and choreography by Fokine, was first performed on June 25, 1910. The dancers experienced difficulty in rehearsal because of the unfamiliar style of some of the music, but the performance went well and was hailed by audience and press as perhaps the best and most exciting work yet offered by the Diaghilev troupe.

Stravinsky already had an idea for another ballet, this one to portray pagan rites in prehistoric Russia, and after the success of *The Firebird* he mentioned his idea to Diaghilev, who urged him to proceed immediately and aim for a production the following spring. After the Paris season ended, Stravinsky went for a short vacation to St. Nazaire, then with his family to Switzerland, first to Vevey and then to Lausanne. He intended to begin work on *The Rite of Spring* (*Le Sacre du printemps*), but what happened was something quite different. In his own words:

> Before tackling the *Sacre du Printemps,* which would be a long and difficult task, I wanted to refresh myself by composing an orchestral piece in which the piano would play the most important part—a sort of *Konzertstück.* In composing the music, I had in my mind a distinct picture of a puppet, suddenly endowed with life, exasperating the patience of the orchestra with diabolical cascades of *arpeggi.* The orchestra in turn retaliates with menacing trumpet-blasts. The outcome is a terrific noise which reaches its climax and ends in the sorrowful and querulous collapse of the poor puppet. Having finished this bizarre piece, I struggled for hours,

while walking beside Lake Geneva, to find a title which would express in a word the character of my music and consequently the personality of this creature.

One day I leapt for joy. I had indeed found my title—*Petroushka*, the immortal and unhappy hero of every fair in all countries. Soon afterwards Diaghileff came to visit me at Clarens,[2] where I was staying. He was much astonished when, instead of sketches of the *Sacre*, I played him the piece which I had just composed and which later became the second scene of *Petroushka*. He was so much pleased with it that he would not leave it alone and began persuading me to develop the theme of the puppet's sufferings and make it into a whole ballet. While he remained in Switzerland we worked out together the general lines of the subject and the plot in accordance with ideas which I suggested. We settled the scene of action: the fair, with its crowd, its booths, the little traditional theatre, the character of the magician, with all his tricks; and the coming to life of the dolls—Petroushka, his rival, and the dancer—and their love tragedy, which ends with Petroushka's death. I began at once to compose the first scene of the ballet.[3]

Diaghilev chose Alexandre Benois (1870–1928) to do the scenario and décor, and again his choice was a fortunate one. A long-time associate of Diaghilev in Russia, it had been he who had been instrumental in persuading the latter to include ballet on the Parisian programs and had done the décor for many of the first productions. There had been a quarrel during the 1910 season when Diaghilev had attributed the plot of *Scheherazade* to Bakst, even though it had been Benois' invention, and Benois had left the company. But Diaghilev knew that his old friend was the logical person to write and mount the proposed new ballet, because of his unique talents and background, and he paid him a reconciliatory visit in St. Petersburg. Benois, once he heard of the new proposal, needed little urging to set to work on a subject so dear to his heart. As he explained:

> Petrouchka, the Russian Guignol or Punch, no less than Harlequin, had been my friend since my earliest childhood. Whenever I heard the loud, nasal cries of the travelling Punch and Judy showman: "Here's Petrouchka! Come, good people, and see the Show!" I would get into a kind of frenzy to see the enchanting performance, which consisted, as did the *balagani* [4]

2. In his *Expositions and Developments*, Garden City, N. Y., 1962, p. 153, Stravinsky corrects this to Lausanne.

3. Igor Stravinsky, *An Autobiography*, New York, 1936, pp. 31–32. Reprinted by permission of Igor Stravinsky.

4. These were traveling showmen, who gave puppet and pantomime shows at fairs and festivals, often featuring Petrushka, the Russian equivalent of Punch.

pantomimes, in the endless tricks of an idle loafer, who ends up by being captured by a hairy devil and dragged off to Hell.

As to Petrouchka in person, I immediately had the feeling that "it was a duty I owed to my old friend" to immortalise him on the real stage. I was still more tempted by the idea of depicting the Butter Week Fair on the stage, the dear *balagani* which were the great delight of my childhood, and had been the delight of my father before me. The fact that in 1911 the *balagani* had, for some ten years, ceased to exist, made the idea of building a kind of memorial to them still more tempting. They perished under the onslaught led by Prince A. P. Oldenburg against alcoholism (the common folk certainly gave themselves up to the Russian Vodka-Bacchus at the Butter Week Fair!).

Besides the duty I felt I owed to Petrouchka and my wish to "immortalise" the St. Petersburg Carnival, I had yet another reason for accepting Seriozha's [5] offer—I suddenly *saw* how this ballet ought to be presented. It at once became plain that Guignol-Petrouchka screens were not appropriate to a stage performance. A year before we had tried to arrange a similar Petrouchka performance with real people in the Arts Club, but although Dobuzhinsky had put much of his wit into the production, it turned out to be rather absurd and on the dull side. The effect of big, grown-up people acting with their heads over the edge of a curtain and little wooden legs dangling below, was more pitiful than funny. The effect on the stage of a real theatre would have been still worse; a ballet would have been entirely out of the question, for what could a ballet artist do if he were not allowed to use his "natural" legs? Once the screens were abolished from the stage, they had naturally to be replaced by a small theatre. The dolls of this theatre would have to come to life without ceasing to be dolls—retaining, so to speak, their doll's nature.

The dolls should come to life at the command of a magician, and their coming to life should be somehow accompanied by suffering. The greater the contrast between the real, live people and the automatons who had just been given life, the sharper the interest of the action would be. It would be necessary to allot a considerable part of the stage to the mass of real people—the "public" at the fair—while there would only be two dolls, the hero of the play, Petrouchka, and his lady.

Soon I decided that there should be a third character—the Blackamoor. In the street performances of Petrouchka there was invariably a separate intermezzo, inserted between the acts: two Blackamoors, dressed in velvet and gold, would appear and start unmercifully hitting each other's wooden heads with sticks. I included a similar Blackamoor among my "chief characters." If Petrouchka were to be taken as the personification of the spiritual and suffering side of humanity—or shall we call it the poetical principle?—his lady Columbine would be the incarnation of the eternal feminine; then the gorgeous Blackamoor would serve as the embodiment of everything senselessly attractive, powerfully masculine and undeservedly triumphant.

5. The nickname by which Diaghilev was known to his friends.

Having once visualised the complete drama in my mind's eye, and foresee-ing what an interesting collision of contrasted elements must inevitably en-sue, how could I refuse Seriozha's proposal that I should help to interpret it as a ballet on the stage? [6]

By now Stravinsky had the score well under way, in Beaulieu where he had moved in October. In December he went to St. Petersburg to visit his mother and work with Benois, who was fascinated and delighted with the parts of the music that the composer played for him on an old drawing-room piano.

The *Russian Dance* proved to be really magic music in which infectious, diabolical recklessness alternated with strange digressions into tenderness—then, after a culminating paroxysm, came to an abrupt end. As for *Petrouchka's Cry,* having listened to it about three times, I began to discern in it grief, and rage, and love, as well as the helpless despair that domi-nated it.[7]

After Stravinsky's departure, the two continued work with mounting en-thusiasm, keeping in touch by letter. Benois was living in a room above an apartment used by the coachmen of a certain Count Bobrinsky, and the sounds of revelry from below helped keep him in a proper frame of mind for certain sections of the scenario.

The early spring of 1911 found the Diaghilev troupe in Rome for performances at the Costanzi Theater during the International Exhibition of that year, and in late April Stravinsky and Benois came there to com-plete the work and begin rehearsals. These were held in the restaurant in the basement of the theater, with the composer accompanying from his not-quite-completed manuscript. The weather was unbearably hot, the floor was covered with a filthy crimson cloth, many details of the stage action had not yet been worked out, many of the dancers were dubious about the music (including Michel Fokine, who was doing the choreog-raphy); yet rehearsals went well, amid a general feeling of mounting enthusiasm for the work. When the company moved to Paris for the spring season, the new work was well under way, and the scenario had been worked out as follows:

Scene I. (*The Admiralty Square, St. Petersburg, during the 1830's. It is a sunny winter's day, and the scene shows a corner of the Shrove-tide*

6. Alexandre Benois, *Reminiscences of the Russian Ballet,* transl. by Mary Britnieva, London, 1941, pp. 324–26. Reprinted by permission of the publisher, Putnam & Company, Ltd.

7. Benois, *Reminiscences,* pp. 327–28. Reprinted by permission.

Fair. In the background, a glimpse of roundabouts, swings and a helter-skelter. On the left, a booth with a balcony for the 'Died' [the barker of the fair]. Beneath it, a table with a large samovar. In the centre, the Showman's little theatre. On the right, sweetmeat stalls and a peepshow.) Crowds of people are strolling about the scene—common people, gentlefolk, a group of drunkards arm-in-arm, children clustering round the peepshow, women round the stalls. A street musician appears with a hurdy-gurdy. He is accompanied by a dancer. Just as she starts to dance, a man with a musical box and another dancer turn up on the opposite side of the stage. After performing simultaneously for a short while, the rivals give up the struggle and retire. Suddenly the Showman comes out through the curtains of the little theatre. The curtains are drawn back to reveal three puppets on their stands—Petrushka, the Ballerina and the Blackamoor. He charms them into life with his flute, and they begin to dance—at first jigging on their hooks in the little theatre, but then, to the general astonishment, stepping down from the theatre and dancing among the public in the open.

Scene II. *(Petrushka's Cell. The cardboard walls are painted black, with stars and a crescent moon upon them. Devils painted on a gold ground decorate the panels of the folding doors that lead into the Ballerina's Cell. On one of the walls is a portrait of the Showman scowling.)* While the Showman's magic has imbued all three puppets with human feelings and emotions, it is Petrushka who feels and suffers most. Bitterly conscious of his ugliness and grotesque appearance, he feels himself to be an outsider, and he resents the way he is completely dependent on his cruel master. He tries to console himself by falling in love with the Ballerina. She visits him in his cell, and for a moment he believes he has succeeded in winning her. But she is frightened by his uncouth antics and flees. In his despair, he curses the Showman and hurls himself at his portrait, but succeeds only in tearing a hole through the cardboard wall of his cell.

Scene III. *(The Blackamoor's Cell. The wall-paper is patterned with green palm-trees and fantastic fruits on a red ground. On the right, a door leading into the Ballerina's cell.)* The Blackamoor, clad in a magnificent costume, is lying on a divan, playing with a coconut. Though he is brutal and stupid, the Ballerina finds him most attractive and successfully uses her wiles to captivate him. Their love-scene is interrupted by the sudden arrival of Petrushka, furiously jealous. He is thrown out by the Blackamoor.

Scene IV. *(The Fair, as in Scene I.)* It is evening, and the festivities have reached their height. A group of wet-nurses dance together. A peasant playing a pipe crosses the stage leading a performing bear. A bibulous merchant, accompanied by two gypsies, scatters handfuls of banknotes among the crowd. A group of coachmen strike up a dance and are joined by the nurses. Finally a number of masqueraders—including devil, goat and pig—rush on to the scene while Bengal flares are let off in the wings.

At this moment there is a commotion in the Showman's theatre. The rivalry between the puppets has taken a fatal turn. Petrushka rushes out from behind the curtain, pursued by the Blackamoor whom the Ballerina tries to restrain. The Blackamoor strikes down Petrushka with his scimitar.

It begins to snow; and Petrushka dies, surrounded by the astonished crowd. (In the commotion the Blackamoor and Ballerina have disappeared.) The Showman is fetched, and he reassures the bystanders that Petrushka is nothing more than a puppet with a wooden head and a body stuffed with sawdust. The crowd disperses as the night grows darker, and the Showman is left behind. But as he starts to drag the puppet off the stage, he is startled to see Petrushka's ghost appear on the roof of the little theatre, jeering and mocking at everyone whom the Showman has fooled.[8]

Rehearsals were held on the stage of the Paris Opera, and they went slowly at first because of problems that the dancers were encountering with the music. Fokine recounts this:

It was necessary to explain the musical counts to the dancers. At times it was especially difficult to remember the rapid changes of the counts. When I went to the rehearsal everything seemed clear. I remembered the music, not only by heart, but I also retained in my head a visual image of the pages and the lines which contained the difficult passages for the dancers. However, the dancers did not look at the music and had to remember everything by ear. It was necessary to stop continually and make excursions into mathematics. At times this disorganized the calm atmosphere of the rehearsal. The mistakes made by the dancers in counting retarded the progress of the work.

* * *

Musically, by far the most difficult part for the dancers in this ballet is the Finale. After the appearance of the masqueraders, the 5/8 count is played at a very rapid pace. This was so difficult to grasp that my rehearsal changed into a lesson in rhythmics. I summoned the troupe to the piano and asked them all to clap their hands. Everyone clapped, but on a different beat. The result was general confusion, so we tried again. I would clap first, then the others would follow me. Then the dancers would clap without me. Many times the pianist would instinctively nod her head. She was anxious to assist the dancers. I requested her not to "conduct with the nose." The dancers would have to dance by themselves without expecting assistance and without watching anyone, including the orchestra conductor and the pianist.

Finally we achieved our objective. But when we applied the acquired rhythms to the dances, nothing happened. Again I recalled everyone to the piano. Again a lesson in rhythms—and so on. In such a manner, very gradually, we finally mastered it.[9]

8. Quoted from Eric Walter White, *Stravinsky: The Composer and His Music,* London and Berkeley, 1966, pp. 158–59; reprinted by permission of the author and Faber and Faber Ltd. White's version is based on a conflation of the outline synopsis and general note that are printed in the 1911 score.

9. Michel Fokine, *Memoirs of a Ballet Master,* transl. by Vitale Fokine, Boston, 1961, pp. 185–86, 187–88. Copyright © 1961 by Vitale Fokine; with permission of Little, Brown and Company.

The sets and costumes arrived from St. Petersburg, where they had been executed by Anisfeld, and the orchestra, under Monteux, began to rehearse; some of the instrumentalists were resentful of the curious sounds they were asked to make. Dress rehearsal was a shambles. Benois was suffering from an abscess on his arm and memories of past indignities. When he noticed that a portrait of the Magician (Showman), which he had painted to be hung on the wall of the puppets' cell, had been altered (it had been damaged and Diaghilev, who had not liked it anyway, had asked Bakst to repaint it), he shouted his displeasure, threw a portfolio of sketches for the ballet on the floor, and rushed out of the theater, not to be seen for days. And there were other problems:

> There were as usual a good many hitches, due chiefly to the fact that the music as played by the orchestra sounded strange to the dancers, and to the necessity of changing the scenery in complete darkness, with large numbers of people on the stage. To make this latter problem worse, Stravinsky had four huge drums set in the prompt corner, which went into action throughout these changes of scene. Moreover, Stravinsky and Fokine had repeated disputes over the *tempi* of the music; the dancers complained that with all the apparatus of the fair they had no room on stage to move; and in the absence of Benois the lighting got out of hand.[10]

But all such difficulties were forgotten after the immediate and unqualified success of the first performance at the Théâtre du Châtelet on June 13. The first criticism of it appeared in the June 17 issue of *Le Figaro,* written by Robert Brussel:

> It is an extraordinary spectacle which must be seen and heard. This young composer, whom lavish nature has endowed with the most rare talents, has begun his career in a fashion with which composers usually end theirs, with a mastery *quasi-exclusive* of the working out of a composition. * * * An extraordinarily colorful, varied and inventive orchestration and a sense of musical movement and stage movement, one as fine as the other, bring about this miracle of equilibrium. *Petrushka* would not have required anything more than a superficial picturesqueness, no doubt, but the talent of M. Stravinsky has imbued the work with far more than mere quaintness.

Jacques Rivière, reviewing the first performance for the September issue of *La nouvelle revue française,* was even more enthusiastic:

10. S. L. Grigoriev, *The Diaghilev Ballet, 1909–1929,* London, 1953, p. 54. Reprinted by permission of the publisher, Constable and Company Ltd.

Petrushka must be called a masterpiece, one of the most unexpected, most impulsive, most buoyant and lively that I know. * * * The music is by Igor Stravinsky; this name, that we have come to know through *The Firebird,* we will never forget now. This young musician knows and handles our modern orchestra, which has become so complex and overburdened, with facility. But he no longer seeks to become more and more complicated, like others; he does not wish to be original by means of minute relationships, of audacious fragments, of fragile and unstable harmonic equilibriums. To the contrary, his audacity is marked by simplification of means (in *Petrushka* there is an interlude consisting of nothing but loud strokes on a drum) .

And M. D. Calvocoressi, one of Stravinsky's earliest champions, first wrote of *Petrushka* in the *Comoedia Illustre* for July 11, 1911:

Even better than *The Firebird, Petrushka* is the work which continues the series of the most characteristic masterpieces of the Russian school. * * * Very refined yet bold even to the smallest detail, the music of *Petrushka* is at the same time quite muscular, of a remarkable sureness of line, of an intensity, of matchless color. There is nothing tentative, nothing unnecessary, nothing forced in the humor or emotion; in short, it is a masterful work and a delightful one.

An account of the birth of *Petrushka,* then, reads like an uninterrupted success story. As Prince Peter Lieven put it:

There are certain undertakings which seem to be conceived, to grow and mature under the guidance of some special providence; everything seems to succeed, every element to merge in one beautiful whole. * * * It is difficult to believe from seeing and hearing *Petrushka* that this ballet was the result of a collective creative impulse. Rather does it seem as if a single super-genius, equally gifted in music, art, painting, and choreography, had conceived, devised, and staged this ballet. It is, of course, the greatest achievement of the *Ballets-Russes,* their admitted masterpiece.[11]

The principal roles were danced by Karsavina (as the Ballerina) , Orloff (the Moor) , Enrico Cecchetti (the Magician) , and of course Nijinsky as Petrushka. A special word should be said about the contribution of the latter. This introverted, silent, moody, mystical person lived so completely within himself that most people who had any contact with him had the impression of a childish, semi-literate person whose success was due to purely physical ability. As each new ballet was being prepared,

11. Prince Peter Lieven, *The Birth of Ballets-Russes,* London, 1936, pp. 130–31. Reprinted by permission of the publisher, George Allen and Unwin Ltd.

those working with him feared that he was not grasping his role, because he went through rehearsals in a mechanical way; but with the first performance he would burst to life and bring to his part the drama and subtlety of interpretation which had been fermenting all along in his brooding mind. His schooling had been in traditional ballet, and *Petrushka,* with its pantomime and emphasis on non-traditional dancing and movement, was something quite new to him. Yet he brought such intensity and pathos to the part of the puppet that Sarah Bernhardt is reputed to have said, after seeing him in the role, "I'm afraid, I'm afraid —because I have just seen the greatest actor in the world."

Despite its success, Diaghilev was reluctant at first to perform *Petrushka* outside of the special world of Paris. It was not offered in Berlin, Vienna, or Budapest, which the troupe visited during the winter of 1911– 12. It was done in Monte Carlo in early 1912, but again Diaghilev decided against doing it on a tour of Germany in the autumn of 1912. Grigoriev gives the following account of its first performance outside of France, in January of 1913:

> We had rather an unpleasant experience in Vienna. Diaghilev had supposed that by now it would be safe to show *Petrushka* there, since after all Vienna was supposed to be musically advanced. At the first orchestral rehearsal, however, the musicians, despite Stravinsky's presence, pronounced the music 'dirty' (whatever this may have meant) and declared they would not play it: it should receive no hearing, they said, within the sacred walls of the Vienna Opera! What had happened was soon known all over the city, and did us no good. We managed indeed to perform *Petrushka,* but only twice; and on each occasion the players duly tried their hand at sabotage.[12]

But the ballet found a warm welcome, indeed almost a second home, in England. Diaghilev had first brought his troupe across the Channel in June of 1911, giving his first program in connection with the coronation of King George V and staying until the end of July. Seven of the most successful ballets were given; in deference to what he supposed English taste to be, Diaghilev chose not to do the two Stravinsky pieces, offering instead such favorites as *Les Sylphides, Prince Igor,* and *Le Spectre de la rose.* Thomas Beecham, who had been instrumental in arranging this first season in England, was employed as a guest conductor. London had seen

12. Grigoriev, *Diaghilev Ballet,* p. 78. Reprinted by permission.

individual Russian dancers before (Karsavina in 1909, Pavlova and Mordkin in 1911), but it was hardly prepared for the vitality, color, excitement, and spectacle of the Ballets Russes. The reception was enthusiastic, and arrangements were hastily made for a return engagement in the fall. The company gave at least one season in London every year after this (except for the war years) until its demise.

For the season of 1912, Diaghilev decided to risk *The Firebird;* its success encouraged him to try *Petrushka* the following year. This first London performance took place at Covent Garden on February 4, with Pierre Monteux conducting; the cast was the same as that of the first Paris performance, except that Orlov had been replaced by Kotchetovsky in the role of the Moor. The notice in the London *Times* was enthusiastic but cautious:

> It is all horribly *macabre* and extraordinarily effective. * * * The whole thing is refreshingly new and refreshingly Russian, more Russian, in fact, than any ballet we have seen. * * * The employment of Russian folk music in the scene in the fair is also most refreshing, and the way in which persistent rhythms bring out the character and movement of the crowd is something quite new. The orchestration is very brilliant throughout, a piano, xylophone, and celesta being employed as well as the usual orchestra. The ballet was very favourably received, though the house seemed a little puzzled by the newness of it all.

But any puzzlement quickly passed, and *Petrushka* was soon regarded by critics and audiences alike as the finest production of the troupe. It was performed on almost every English season of the Ballets Russes, right through the final engagement in 1929. English intellectuals took the tragic puppet to heart, and some of the finest literature on the ballet has come from their pens.

With the outbreak of World War I, it became increasingly difficult for the Diaghilev company to find engagements in Europe, and there was much discussion of bringing the Ballets Russes to the New World. This dream became a reality when the company, over 70 strong, sailed on the French liner *Lafayette* on January 1, 1916, and arrived in New York on the 11th, hailed by the American press with an almost unprecedented barrage of publicity. Lengthy articles on the history of the troupe, photographs, and interviews with Diaghilev and some of the dancers filled the daily and Sunday papers and even crowded the war off the front pages.

Diaghilev's plan was to open with some of his most successful productions, but to sustain interest by reserving several of his very best shows for the second and third weeks. Thus audiences saw *The Afternoon of a Faun, Prince Igor, Scheherazade,* and *The Firebird* the first week, but *Petrushka* was not staged until the second, receiving its first American performance on January 24, 1916, at the Century Theatre.

New York audiences and critics were as dazzled by the sights and sounds of Russian ballet as those in London. Less experienced and less critical than Europeans, they were not bothered at first by the absence of a number of the best dancers (most notably Karsavina and Nijinsky), by the fact that some of the stage decorations were not as elaborate as they had expected, and by some weaknesses in the orchestra. New York had never witnessed anything quite like this. *The Firebird* made the strongest impression the first week; this was the first performance of a major Stravinsky work in this country, it should be remembered.

But suddenly there was trouble. The Catholic Theater Movement issued a "White List" bulletin directed at Diaghilev, a solemn document beginning: "In a most subtle manner and under many guises indecency upon the stage is exploited and made profitable." There was strong complaint against sections of two ballets: the gestures of the faun at the end of *The Afternoon of a Faun* and the orgy scene involving slaves (black) of the Sultan and the young women (white) of the harem in *Scheherazade.* Controversy over the first was an old story by now, but only in America had there been objection to the second. The Third Deputy Police Commissioner immediately ordered a conference of interested parties, including Diaghilev, John Brown (business manager of the Metropolitan Opera House, which was sponsoring the troupe in New York), and Alfred Seligsberg, counsel for the Ballets Russes. Newspapers reported that agreement to modify subsequent performances was reached "amicably"; the faun was to content himself with gazing at the veil dropped by the nymph, and the slaves were to be made up a light gray. After the next performance of these works, Diaghilev was reported by the *New York Times* to have walked down the aisle from his seat in the orchestra circle saying loudly, "America is saved!"

But with the first performance of *Petrushka,* on January 24, such matters were forgotten as excitement over the Russian troupe mounted even higher. Ansermet conducted, with only Cecchetti of the original cast dancing the role he had created; Lydia Lopokova took the role of the Ballerina, Leonide Massine was Petrushka, and Adolf Bolm was cast as the Moor. There was almost unanimous agreement in the press that the piece was a masterpiece. The music struck American ears as harsh, complex, and difficult, but there was agreement that this was just the sort of music needed for such a piece. All in all, critics in New York (and later in other American cities) passed remarkably fair and perceptive judgement on *Petrushka,* even though it was quite different from the music they knew best. Some of the most penetrating and cogent discussions of the work were written by American critics on the occasion of their first hearing and viewing of it.

For example, the *New York Times* reported on January 25:

> Petrouchka * * * is altogether one of the most extraordinary products of the contemporary Russian school, both in its pictorial effects—the phantasmagoria of color, of Russian carnival characters, costumes, and boisterous action—and in its music, equally a phantasmagoria of incomparable verve and brilliancy, fitting and illustrating in every detail for the ear what is presented to the eye. Both are of indescribable fascination. * * * The piece, with all its exaggerated grotesquerie and burlesque features in the music—music that would be wholly unintelligible, useless, and tedious apart from each single detail of the accompanying action—evidently made a deep impression upon the public, an impression of amusement and exhilaration.

Other critics echoed virtually the same sentiments. The *Sun's* critic said:

> Stravinsky's music is delicious. If it were performed as a concert piece it would give rise to all sorts of learned debate and men would sit up till small hours arguing with each other about it. Heard in connection with the action for which it was designed, it becomes a string of glittering gems of burlesque humor. * * * This arena of the humorous ballet is a fine field for the futurist composer. Stravinsky has that sense of humor which permits him to employ the latest solemn devices in harmony and instrumentation to evoke a smile. It is a grace often wanting, and when found it should be welcomed.

The music obviously fell less easily on American ears than it had on European, as almost every critic pointed out. The review of the first performance in *Musical America,* which appeared in the issue of January 29, said, "As far as Stravinsky's music goes, there are times when its terrible dissonances almost strain one's nerves, but it is all so original, and so absolutely effective in accompanying the burlesque and comedy of the action as to make it wholly inimitable," and the critic of the *World* found that "the weird color of the score, which shrieked dissonance in every manner possible to the modern composer, was amazingly appropriate." But strange as some of the music seemed to American audiences and critics, they were quite willing to accept the score for what it was. These first American reviews are fascinating documents, attesting to a flexibility of taste and a willingness to accept something unusual that have unfortunately not always been characteristic of American criticism since 1916. A portion of still another review of the first *Petrushka* in America, this one from the *Musical Courier* for February 3, will serve as a summary of the reception of the work in New York:

> Heard alone, most of it would undoubtedly be extremely ugly, though there is a dance or two so filled with true musical humor as to be quite capable of separate hearing as absolute music; heard in connection with the doings on the stage, one quite forgets the eccentricities of the music in admiration of its fittingness. The more one hears of Stravinsky's music, the surer one is that this man is not only a strong talent, but already far on the road to being a genius.

Now the company embarked on a tour of the East and Midwest. Boston was first, the first week in February. There was no scandal, though Diaghilev reinstated the "objectionable" sequences in the several ballets, and special police were on hand in anticipation. Audiences were large, but somewhat cool at first, and the press carried comments on the missing star dancers and the attitude of some members of the company toward playing in the "provinces." But *Petrushka* again aroused great excitement, and was the most successful and highly praised production. Boston critics distinguished themselves in their notices of the work; indeed, an account and criticism of it by H. T. Parker, which appeared in the *Boston Evening Transcript,* is one of the finest appreciations of *Petrushka* ever written (see p. 195).

Albany was next, for one night, then Detroit and Chicago. The reception of the company, and of *Petrushka* in particular, was enthusiastic at first, though the further inland Stravinsky's music penetrated, the harsher it seemed to sound. It was given its first Chicago performance on February 18, and Charles E. Watts said of it in the *Music News* for February 25:

> Much as the reviewer dislikes personally the ultramodern music, it remains as a paradox that he is absolutely fascinated with the two pieces by Stravinsky he has heard. "Petrouchka" is, without doubt, the most remarkable piece of work ever presented by any ballet company in Chicago. * * *

[The music] is merely a succession of fearsome sounds so utterly outre and ridiculous as to incite continuous laughter on its own accord, while it also evokes much respect for the skill of those who play it. Particularly difficult and equally hideous is the piano score, and yet the whole thing is fascinating.

The success of *Petrushka* in Chicago was marred by a storm of criticism that broke in the press over the allegedly "licentious" nature of several of the productions. Damaging publicity preceded the troupe to Milwaukee, but the episode was gradually forgotten during the course of performances in various of the larger midwestern cities (St. Paul–Minneapolis, Kansas City, St. Louis, Indianapolis, Cincinnati, Cleveland, and Pittsburgh). The company swung back east, climaxing the tour with a four-week season at the Metropolitan Opera House that began sluggishly but built to a peak of excitement with the first American performances by Nijinsky. The great dancer had been in an Austrian detention camp since the outbreak of the war; upon his release, he joined the troupe and on April 12, 1916, danced for the first time in this country, in two of his finest roles, in *Petrushka* and *Le Spectre de la rose.*

The next season, the Ballets Russes returned to America for an even longer tour. After a mid-October opening in New York, the company of fifty-five dancers, fifty-two musicians, and a large technical and promotional staff, boarded the Russian Ballet Special for a transcontinental tour.

November was spent on the East Coast, with performances in such medium-sized and even smallish towns as New Haven, Worcester, Hartford, and Bridgeport. The company headed south (Richmond, Atlanta, New Orleans), reached Texas (Dallas, Houston), turned up into the lower Midwest (Wichita, Des Moines), then west (Denver, Salt Lake City). Christmas was spent in California (Los Angeles, Hollywood). After a brief rest, they went up the Pacific Coast (Fresno, Sacramento, Seattle, Vancouver), started back east (Fargo, Duluth), swung down through the Midwest again (performing at most of the cities they had visited the previous year as well as such new ones as Dayton, Toledo, Buffalo, and Toronto), and finally ended back in the East in mid-February, four months and forty cities after the tour had begun. The Russians had performed for cowboys, ex-slaves, Indians, Mormons, movie stars, miners, and assorted other Americans, most of whom had had no previous contact with ballet of any sort.

Petrushka was performed in many of these cities, though not all of them. Thus Americans first came to know the work as a ballet, within a few years of its creation, and they reacted to it and evaluated it as a work of art in which music, dance, and the visual arts were component parts of the total work. It was accepted, and remembered, as a dramatic work, and many Americans responded to the tragic puppet in as emotional a way as had the English. Here is one small bit of testimony, taken from the program notes of the first concert performance in St. Louis, written by a man (Harry R. Burke) still thinking of the work as the drama he had seen danced and pantomimed by the Russians:

> Was the original "Petrouchka" a symbol of the Russian people in the hands of their rulers, as has been hinted? * * * It is a terrible indictment of human life—this music—in that perspective. The callous crowd, gawking, avid for pleasure, brutal in its orgies, is quite as pitiful as is the puppet. And the beautiful Ballerina, crying herself for sympathy, is not less callous than the crowd when Petrouchka offers love. But one man has so summed up in words, a criticism of the human struggle, from years of disillusion, loneliness and bitterness. That man was once a St. Louisan. People knew him by the name "Mark Twain."

It was not until memories of the Ballets Russes faded and *Petrushka* became popular concert and recording fare in the 1940s and 1950s that discussion shifted to the music itself. It has become familiar to millions of Americans now, and it is possible to listen to it today as a succession of cheerful, vigorous, even quaint bits of musical tapestry. We have found terms to label the musical devices that bewildered some listeners sixty years ago and can give a more convincing technical account of what happens in the piece than anyone could have then. But perhaps we can learn something from the early reviewers by reading what they have to say of *Petrushka,* of how the piece came to life on the stage and touched the audience in ways that much music of today does not even attempt.

Petrushka stayed in the repertory of the Ballets Russes until the troupe was disbanded following Diaghilev's death in 1929. Nijinsky, the first and greatest interpreter of the title role, made his last appearance in the work on September 26, 1917. It had been obvious for some time that he was deteriorating, mentally and emotionally, and he was soon in an asylum where he would spend the remainder of his days, suffering from what was diagnosed as schizophrenia.

A decade later it was decided to see what response, if any, he would have to a performance of the work which he had helped create and had danced so many times. He was brought to a performance of *Petrushka* at the Opéra in Paris on December 27, 1928. Sitting in a box with Diaghilev, he watched and listened attentively, but spoke only in answer to a direct question. Afterwards he was brought on stage to meet the cast, and a photograph was taken of him surrounded by Diaghilev, Benois, Karsavina, Grigoriev, and other former colleagues. He greeted them with a vacant smile, but would not come out of his private world. He was never to see another ballet.

The orchestral score for *Petrushka* was published in Berlin by the Russischer Musikverlag in 1912, as was a transcription for piano, four hands. In 1921 Stravinsky prepared an arrangement of portions of the work for piano, to "provide piano virtuosi with a piece having sufficient scope to enable them to add to their modern repertory and display their technique"; this was titled *Trois mouvements de Petrouchka*. A miniature orchestral score appeared in 1922; T. Szántó arranged for piano a suite of five pieces from the work in 1923; and Stravinsky and Samuel Dushkin transcribed the *Russian Dance* of the first tableau for violin and piano in 1933. All these were published by the Russischer Musikverlag.

Loopholes in international copyright law made it possible for *Petrushka* to be "pirated" in the United States, and partly for this reason Stravinsky rewrote the piece in 1947 for publication by Boosey and Hawkes. The new *Petrushka* is quite different from the old: it is scored for a somewhat smaller orchestra; the rhythmic notation has been simplified, and at the same time made more precise, so that less freedom of execution is left to the performers; in many places, accompanimental patterns supporting the primary melody have been rewritten to have more contrapuntal interest; and it is obviously designed now as a concert piece, with stage directions almost completely eliminated and an optional loud ending put in for conductors who like pieces to end with a bang. Suggested performance time is 42 minutes, to 33 for the original. Both versions are performed today, and there has been discussion of the relative merits of the two. *Petrushka* of 1911 and *Petrushka* of 1947 are indeed two rather different pieces, and any historical study of the work, any analysis of it that attempts to demonstrate why it had such a profound effect on audiences and composers in the first part of the century must of course be based on the earlier, original version.

Though the first concert performance of *Petrushka* took place only a few years after the premiere of the ballet—on March 1, 1914, in the

concert series at the Casino de Paris, with Pierre Monteux conducting—
it did not become popular concert fare for some years. The first performance in Boston was on November 26, 1920, at a concert of the
Boston Symphony Orchestra under Monteux; Cincinnati first heard it
during the 1924–25 season, under Stravinsky; it was first done in Phila-
delphia in 1926–27, in St. Louis in the fall of 1928, and in Chicago in
1930. Sometimes the entire score of the ballet was performed, but more
often only selections from the score were played. Stravinsky himself made
a suite from it, which he conducted in the 1920s, but this was never
published, and other conductors often arranged their own suites from
Petrushka. At first, the specter of the ballet peered over the shoulder of
any conductor who undertook to perform the piece in concert. After the
first Boston performance, Jack Coles wrote in the *Musical Courier,* "This
music loses in effect when transferred from the theater to the concert
hall.*** The action of the plot cannot be divorced from the music
without impairing its dramatic effect." But as memories of the Ballets
Russes faded, *Petrushka* was played more and more, becoming in time
one of the very most popular compositions of the 20th century.

THE SCORE
OF PETRUSHKA

4 Flutes (*Fl.* or *Fl. gr.*)
    IV. doubles on Piccolo (*Fl. Picc.*)
4 Oboes (*Ob.*)
    IV. doubles on English horn (*Cor Ingl.*)
4 Clarinets (*Cl.*) in B♭ (*Si♭*) or A (*La*)
    IV. doubles on Bass clarinet (*Cl. basso*)
4 Bassoons (*Fag.*)
    IV. doubles on Contrabassoon (*Cont. F.* or *C. Fag.*)

4 Horns (*Cor.*) in F
2 Cornets (*Pist.*) in B♭ (*Si♭*) or A (*La*)
2 Trumpets (*Tr.*) in B♭ (*Si♭*) or A (*La*)
    I. doubles on Trumpet in D (*Tr. picc. in Re*)
3 Trombones (*Trb.*)
1 Tuba

Timpani (*Timp.*)

Percussion:
    Bass drum (*Gr. Cassa* or *G. Cassa*)
    Cymbals (*Piatti*)
    Gong (*Tam-T.*)
    Triangle (*Trgl.*)
    Tambourine (*Tamb. de Basque*)
    Snare drum (*Tamb. milit.*)
    Xylophone (*Xyloph.*)
    Glockenspiel (*Camp.*)
    Snare drum (*Tamb. milit.*) and Long drum (*Tambourin*) in the wings
2 Harps
Piano
Celesta

Violin I (*V. I*)
Violin II (*V. II*)
Viola
Violoncello (*Cello*)
Double Bass (*C. B.*)

TEXTUAL NOTE

This edition, based on the score published by the Russischer Musikverlag, Berlin, 1912, corrects certain errors that have been found in the course of the years. The majority of these are self-evident engraver's errors, and require no special comment. However, since it occasionally occurs in performance, the following deserves mention: after rehearsal number 111, the bass drum stroke occurs on the third measure, not the second as in previous editions (cf. the analogous place after 110). The publisher is grateful to Professor Claudio Spies, of Swarthmore College, for providing a list of these errors, and to Professor Boris Schwarz, of Queens College, for his assistance in the translation of the original Russian stage directions.

PETRUSHKA

FIRST TABLEAU

THE SHROVE-TIDE FAIR

SPECIAL CURTAIN

ENTERTAINS THE CROWD FROM THE HEIGHT OF HIS BOOTH.

IN THE CROWD APPEARS AN ORGAN-GRINDER WITH A STREET DANCER.

THE ORGAN-GRINDER BEGINS TO PLAY.

THE STREET DANCER DANCES,
13 BEATING TIME ON THE TRIANGLE.

*THE ORGAN-GRINDER, CONTINUING TO TURN THE CRANK WITH ONE HAND, PLAYS
THE CORNET WITH THE OTHER.

AT THE OTHER END OF THE STAGE, A MUSIC BOX PLAYS,

AROUND WHICH ANOTHER STREET DANCER DANCES.

THE FIRST DANCER

AGAIN BEATS THE TRIANGLE.

*THE ORGAN-GRINDER RESUMES PLAYING THE CORNET.

THE MUSIC BOX STOP PLAYING; THE SHOWMAN
AGAIN ATTRACTS THE ATTENTION OF THE CROWD.

THE MERRYMAKERS RETURN.

TWO DRUMMERS, STANDING IN FRONT OF

THE LITTLE THEATER, ATTRACT THE ATTENTION
OF THE CROWD BY THEIR DRUM-ROLLS.

OUT OF THE LITTLE THEATER
STEPS THE OLD MAGICIAN

THE MAGIC TRICK

THE MAGICIAN PLAYS THE FLUTE.

THE CURTAIN OF THE LITTLE THEATER OPENS, AND THE CROWD SEES THREE PUPPETS:
PETRUSHKA, A MOOR, AND A BALLERINA.

THE MAGICIAN ANIMATES THEM BY
TOUCHING THEM WITH HIS FLUTE.

RUSSIAN DANCE

PETRUSHKA, THE MOOR, AND THE BALLERINA BEGIN TO DANCE TOGETHER,
TO THE GREAT SURPRISE OF ALL.

Russian folk song

34

A DORIAN

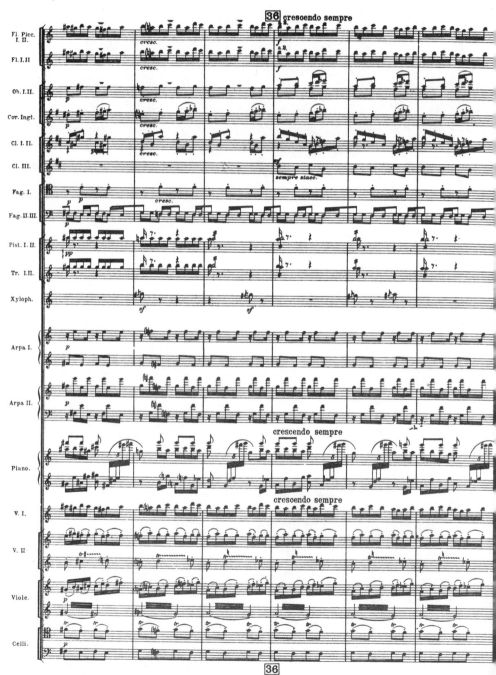

First Tableau

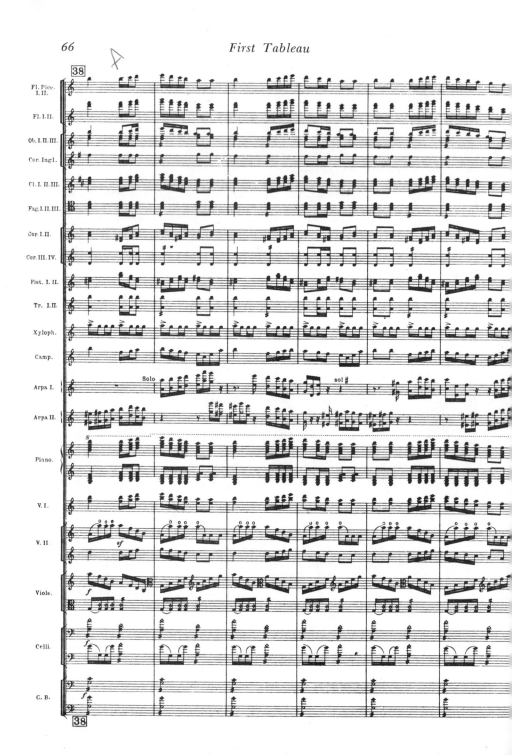

B fragments

DARKNESS. THE CURTAIN FALLS.

*) Son lointain, mais violent. Réglez selon l'acoustique de la sale.

SECOND TABLEAU

PETRUSHKA'S ROOM

AT THE RISE OF THE CURTAIN, THE DOOR OF PETRUSHKA'S ROOM OPENS ABRUPTLY, A FOOT KICKS HIM
ONSTAGE; PETRUSHKA FALLS, AND THE DOOR CLOSES AGAIN.

*)POUR L'EXÉCUTION DE CONCERT CETTE BATTERIE DE TAMBOUR EST SUPPRIMÉE.

79

THIRD TABLEAU

THE MOOR'S ROOM

*) POUR L'EXÉCUTION DE CONCERT CETTE BATTERIE DE TAMBOURS EST SUPPRIMÉE.

94

APPEARANCE OF THE BALLERINA

DANCE OF THE BALLERINA
(CORNET IN HAND)

WALTZ
(THE BALLERINA AND THE MOOR)

QUARREL OF THE MOOR WITH PETRUSHKA. THE BALLERINA FAINTS.

THE MOOR PUSHES PETRUSHKA OUT OF THE DOOR. DARKNESS. CURTAIN.

FOURTH TABLEAU

THE SHROVE-TIDE FAIR

(TOWARDS EVENING)

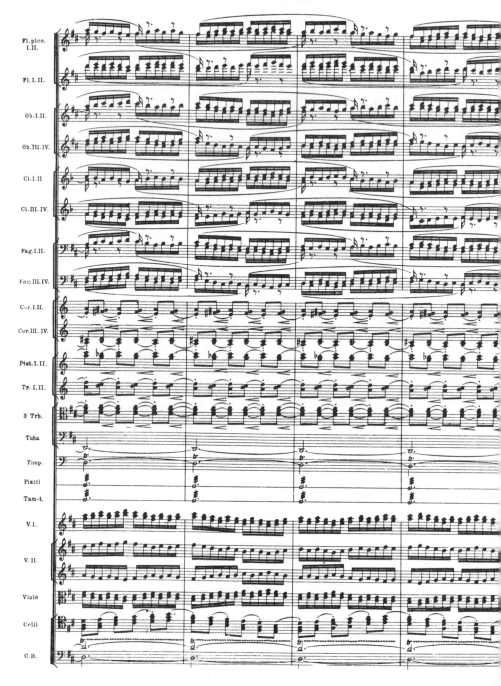

DANCE OF THE NURSEMAIDS

114

A PEASANT ENTERS WITH A BEAR. THE CROWD SCATTER

THE PEASANT PLAYS A PIPE. THE BEAR WALKS ON HIS HIND LEGS.

THE PEASANT WITH THE BEAR GOES AWAY.

A DAPPER MERCHANT BURSTS IN WITH TWO GYPSY GIRLS. IN JOVIAL MERRIMENT, HE TOSSES BANKNOTES
TO THE CROWD.

103 THE GYPSY GIRLS DANCE. THE MERCHANT PLAYS THE ACCORDION.

*) come sopra (sempre)

107 THE MERCHANT AND THE GYPSY GIRLS LEAVE.

DANCE OF THE COACHMEN AND STABLE BOYS

112 THE NURSEMAIDS DANCE WITH THE COACHMEN AND STABLE BOYS.

116

THE MUMMERS

THE DEVIL (A MASKER) FROLICS WITH THE CROWD.

120 JESTING OF THE MUMMERS (THE GOATS AND THE PIGS).

THE MASKERS AND THE MUMMERS DANC

THE REST OF THE CROWD JOINS IN THE DANCE OF THE MUMMERS.

THE CROWD CONTINUES TO DANCE, DISREGARDING
THE CRIES THAT EMERGE FROM THE LITTLE
THEATER.

THE DANCE STOPS. PETRUSHKA DASHES FROM THE THEATER, PURSUED BY THE MOOR, WHOM THE
BALLERINA TRIES TO RESTRAIN.

THE ENRAGED MOOR OVERTAKES HI

AND STRIKES HIM WITH HIS SABER. **PETRUSHKA FALLS,** **A CROWD SURROUNDS PETRUSHKA.**
HIS SKULL BROKEN.

HE DIES PLAINTIVELY. A POLICEMAN IS SENT TO FETCH THE MAGICIAN.

THE MAGICIAN ARRIVES.

HE PICKS UP THE
CORPSE OF PETRUSHK

ABOVE THE LITTLE THEATER APPEARS PETRUSHKA'S GHOST, THREATENING AND
THUMBING HIS NOSE AT THE MAGICIAN.

TERRIFIED, THE MAGICIAN DROPS THE PUPPET
PETRUSHKA FROM HIS HANDS AND, LOOKING
BACK FEARFULLY, HURRIES AWAY.

CURTAIN

L'istesso tempo.   Molto più lento.

ROME 13/26 MAI 1911.

THE MUSIC
OF THE BALLET

The Music of the Ballet

Some critics have seen *Petrushka* as an intermediate work in Stravinsky's development. They see *The Firebird* as the masterly work of his youth, full of his own musical personality yet still deeply and obviously indebted to his teachers and older contemporaries, and the three major works that followed *Petrushka* (*The Rite of Spring, Les Noces,* and *L'Histoire du soldat*) first exhibiting in striking fashion the new compositional techniques that were to have so much influence on other composers in the following decades. Today, however, with the perspective of time in our favor, it is much easier to see all these works as links in a chain, with no break, even at *The Rite.* At the most elementary level, it is a simple matter to go through the score of *Petrushka* and pick out, on the one hand, passages that could not have been written without an intimate knowledge of the music of Mussorgsky, Strauss, Rimsky-Korsakov, and even Debussy, and on the other, passages that clearly presage the next works. Analyses of melodic, rhythmic, harmonic, and orchestral techniques lead to the same conclusions.

Perhaps the unique and most remarkable feature of *Petrushka* is that even though this is true, even though it is possible to isolate widely disparate stylistic elements, the piece nevertheless has a remarkable sense of unity. Everything in the score seems to follow logically, though this logic cannot always be demonstrated by means of musical analysis. The unification is more of personality, or mood, or spirit. The type of logical, disciplined analysis so dear to present-day theorists may tell us many things about many works, but it is not the best tool for such a work as *Petrushka.* The best reviews of early performances of the ballet tell us this, after all; they scarcely mention technical aspects of the composition (though many of the critics were knowledgeable enough to dis-

175

cuss such matters if they had thought it relevant or important enough), but rather the character and effect of the piece. Despite its success, there was some adverse criticism, and, interestingly, this was not directed against specific musical devices, but against the character of the piece, the general mood, which impressed some people as vulgar and flippant, not dignified as "art" music should be. Stravinsky reports that there was particular hostility in Russia, and that Andrei Rimsky-Korsakov questioned his use of such "trash" as Russian popular melodies.[1]

Diaghilev's ballets were regarded as revolutionary because they often abandoned traditional ballet steps and movements for pantomime. In place of set dances, there would be stretches of what might be called narration, or prose dancing. A parallel might be drawn with such operas as Debussy's *Pelléas et Mélisande* and Strauss's *Salome,* which almost completely abandon the "number" principle in favor of freely unfolding, asymmetrical, non-rounded dramatic and musical structures. A characteristic feature of *Petrushka* is the mixture of set dances and narration. There are many dances in which the dramatic action comes to a halt while one or more characters perform a descriptive or lyric dance; such sections are usually accompanied by simple, closed, sectional forms in the music, of the sort that had been used in dance music for many centuries. But just as often the stage action unfolds freely in pantomime and gesture, moving forward without recourse to traditional ballet sequences, and here the music is narrative in shape also, developing ideas without turning back on itself, or repeating musical motives, or shaping itself into traditional musical forms.

Stravinsky's harmonic vocabulary is so large and varied in *Petrushka* that the work could serve as a dictionary of early 20th-century practice. There are simple, diatonic, tonal accompaniments to some of the popular or pseudo-popular tunes, chords built on the whole-tone scale, diatonic chord-clusters, chords built on fifths and octaves, modal harmonizations, chromatic progressions and chromatically altered chords, and harmonic structures built from the superimposition of two different chords from the same or different keys. The most famous chord, used in different ways in various parts of the piece and so characteristic that it has been

---

1. Stravinsky reports this in his *Expositions and Developments*, p. 154. In his *Memories and Commentaries*, Garden City, N. Y., 1960, p. 53, he says that Andrei dismissed *Petrushka* as "Russian vodka with French perfumes" in a review for a Russian journal.

called the "Petrushka chord," results from the simultaneous sounding of two triads a tritone apart, most often C major and F♯ major. It is first heard in two clarinets at 49 [2]; much of the piano part of the second tableau is based on it, with one hand playing on the white keys and the other on the black; it is heard often in this tableau, and in sections of the next two, as the harmonic basis of a dialogue for two trumpets; and the tonal ambiguity implicit in the selection of these two chords is maintained to the very end of the ballet, where the penultimate note is a C and the last an F♯. Stravinsky says that the simultaneous use of two keys was conceived as an insult to the audience by Petrushka, and the use of it at the end of the last tableau shows that his ghost is still insulting them.[3]

Dramatically and visually, the two outer tableaux make a matching pair, as do the inner two. The first and fourth take place in the square, they are the longest, they contain much dancing by the entire crowd or by smaller groups, and the music is often similar in nature, with some use of the same melodic material. The second and third tableaux take place in the puppets' cells, and involve only the three protagonists. Musically, the episode of Petrushka's death (from 125 to the end) comes as a sort of coda, though it is the dramatic climax. Stravinsky's original intention was to have the crowd scenes of this last tableau seen from the perspective of Petrushka's cell, with the puppet watching through a hole in his wall. But it was decided that since the first part of the tableau is the loudest and liveliest section of the entire ballet, it should be brought to the center and front of the stage.

The first tableau breaks into three sections of uneven length: the first, from 1 through 29 in the score, is a scene of crowd activity in Admiralty Square; drum rolls lead to the introduction of the Magician and his puppets, from 30 to 33; and the tableau concludes with a *Russian Dance* by the three puppets, from 33 to 47.

The first section is a characteristic example of Stravinsky's use of traditional, sectional form, in this instance a rondo. We hear first bustling crowd noise, a mist of sound with trills and tremolos in the winds, and rapid running figures in the harps and piano. A fragment of a pentatonic tune is heard immediately in the flute, followed by several other fragments or suggestions of tunes at 2 and 3. The one heard in the lower

2. In my discussion, numbers refer to the rehearsal numbers in the score.
3. Cf. *Expositions and Developments*, p. 156.

instruments at 2 has been identified as a folk song of the Volochebniki in the province of Smolensk,[4] and there may be other actual folk material here also. At 5, the Volochebniki song is taken up by full orchestra in a more extended statement, to accompany a crowd of revelers, and at 7 some of the initial crowd noises reappear. An organ grinder has come on stage, with a dancer, and his music breaks through the general bustle three measures after 9; his simple, sentimental, trite melody is heard clearly at 15, with masterful and witty orchestration suggestive of the tone of the instrument that he pretends to play on stage. He plays a second tune at 13, while the dancer performs for the crowd. This melody is not Stravinsky's, but is taken from a song then popular in Paris, "Elle avait un' jambe en bois."[5] Another dancer appears, with a music box, and the two dance in competition (from 15 to 17) while their two tunes are heard in counterpoint, the music box depicted by bells in the orchestra. The crowd becomes restless; fragments of the original crowd motive intrude on the dance tunes, and at 17 the two dancers are forced to stop as general dancing resumes. The Volochebniki song returns at 20, scored for full orchestra, and at 22 there is another return to the music which was heard at the very beginning, this time extended, developed, and working to a climax just before 29.

The music of this section, then, falls into an ABACABA scheme: A is the original crowd music, B the Volochebniki song, and C the music of the two dancers. The brief scene before the Magician's booth, which follows, is by contrast a narrative section, with continuously unfolding music. Drum rolls quiet the crowd, at 29; the Magician appears, to the accompaniment of chromatic sliding passages in the lower winds and mysterious rustles and flutters from the strings and harp (30); he plays an almost silly cadenza on his flute, at 31; and the mysterious noises are heard again at 32 as the curtain of the puppet theater opens.

The third section, the familiar *Russian Dance*, is danced by the three puppets, who have been brought to life by a touch of the Magician's flute. It is again cast in a simple, sectional form, this time ABABA. A, first

4. For further details about the folk songs used in *Petrushka*, see the article by Frederick W. Sternfeld reprinted below, p. 203.

5. Stravinsky heard this tune played by a hurdy-gurdy beneath his window as he was working on this scene (in Beaulieu) and appropriated it, not realizing that it was a recent tune by a Mr. Spencer, protected by copyright. In consequence, a percentage of the royalties from performances of *Petrushka* went to Mr. Spencer, or his heirs. Stravinsky tells of this episode in *Memories and Commentaries*, pp. 89–90.

stated by full orchestra at 33, is apparently of Stravinsky's invention, but B, first given out in fragmentary form at 34, is a Russian folk song for St. John's Eve. The A theme returns at 37, scored even more heavily; longer fragments of B, played by various solo instruments, are heard in the section beginning at 39, and the tune is finally played in complete form by the piano at 41. A transition built on fragments of A leads to the final statement of this theme, played first by the piano at 43 and then by full orchestra. The dance comes to an abrupt end at 47. Darkness descends on the stage, and a few drum taps and a curious final echo of the crowd music in the oboes lead to the second tableau.

This tableau, the shortest, was the first to be written by Stravinsky. Though he thought of it first as a concert piece for piano and orchestra, it was nevertheless conceived as a dramatic work, a dialogue between the soloist and orchestra, and its structure was determined more by dramatic considerations than by abstract musical factors. In contrast with the first tableau, there are no set dances here, only narrative pantomime and gesture. The music is a sort of patchwork, with short sections of contrasting character succeeding one another, each too brief to allow much development of musical ideas. The tableau can be broken down into a loose ABA form, musically, but to the ear it appears to unfold freely, unified more by recurring melodic and harmonic motives than by any traditional form.

The scene is set in Petrushka's cell; the interior curtain is pulled at 48, and the puppet makes a precipitant entrance, kicked through the door by the Magician, to a short scurry of music. Sliding chromatic passages in the strings reflect his piteous state, as he lies on the floor, and we immediately hear the characteristic tritone relationship that permeates this scene as the upper strings end on a C major chord and the contrabasses follow with an F♯, pizzicato. At 49, we hear for the first time the bitonal arpeggio which Stravinsky says is Petrushka's insult to the audience: the B♭ clarinet outlines a C major triad against an F♯ major triad in the A clarinet. Scurrying arpeggio passages in the piano, culminating in a pseudo-cadenza (all this with the right hand on the white keys and the left on the black), lead to a *furioso* section (51), in which Petrushka shakes his fist at the world and curses it. Strident arpeggios in the brass are supported by busy accompanimental figures in the strings and winds based mostly on the superimposition of C major and F♯ major triads.

The mood changes at 52, with a change of tempo and key; this is the B section. After a tentative beginning, interrupted by another outburst from the piano, a simple, sad tune is stated and repeated. It is in the nature of a folk tune, but is apparently Stravinsky's own.

With the entrance of the Ballerina, at 56, there is a dramatic change of mood. Petrushka is agitated at the sight of his beloved partner, and the orchestra gives out disconnected bits and fragments of motives, almost a jumble of sound. The ear cannot sort out a melodic line, or even underlying harmonic progressions, in this passage, which perplexed some listeners at early performances of the work.

The Ballerina is repelled by his antics, and leaves. Petrushka's outburst subsides in a clarinet cadenza, and then one for the piano. More passage work for the piano at 59 leads to another outburst of despair (at 60) similar in musical material to the *furioso* section earlier. This trails off with subsiding chords at 61, a last bitonal arpeggio from the clarinets, and a final shriek from the cornets and trumpets as the stage is darkened.

Petrushka had been a mere puppet performing a somewhat mechanical dance in the first tableau. In the second we see him experiencing a variety of quite human emotions.

The third tableau takes place in the cell of the Moor, who is first seen reclining on a divan, toying with a coconut. Violent chords built on open fifths, then snarling chromatic passages in the strings suggest his brutal, exotic, even vicious nature. He dances at 65, to a minor tune scored in masterful fashion for two clarinets playing at an interval of two octaves, accompanied by a drone bass and cymbals. Another brilliant stroke of orchestration occurs at 66, where the cellos and basses play in their lowest register, *sul ponticello,* in accompaniment of a chromatic fragment in the English horn. Next come loud chromatic blasts from the brasses (67) and a quiet section with winds in parallel triads against strings and percussion. This section moves somewhat aimlessly from one musical idea to another, like the simple mind of the Moor.

An abbreviated fanfare and a tattoo from the snare drum herald the entrance of the Ballerina, who dances for the Moor to the accompaniment of a simple, trite, mostly triadic tune played by the cornet. The sluggish Moor begins to stir at 70, as the orchestra sounds bits of music reminiscent of the opening of this tableau, and the two dance a waltz, beginning at 71. This is cast in a simple ABA form; Stravinsky borrowed both melodies from Joseph Lanner, the most successful Viennese waltz composer before Strauss.[6] Stravinsky's treatment of these tunes is remarkable, and anticipates what he was to do with borrowed material in later works. On the one hand, he parodies them by the use of such orchestral tricks as the arpeggiated bassoon accompaniment, the overlapping phrases between flute and cornet, the staccato repeated notes in the flute against the legato cornet line, and the silly grace notes in the flute part in the B section. But even though he pokes fun at the musical style that the waltzes represent, he still retains and even emphasizes its essence, the sentimentality that he needs at this point in his drama. The Ballerina dances alone at first, then the Moor joins her (9 measures after 72) as the lowest strings and winds play his heavy, clumsy theme against the graceful flutes and harps. One can hear in the music that she stops her dance for a moment (six measures before 74) while he continues his awkward steps, perhaps unaware that she is no longer dancing with him.

Fragments of some of the Moor's characteristic music are heard at 74, as he urges her to resume the waltz, and at 75 the two dance together again as the orchestra repeats the first of the Lanner waltzes. This time the Moor is portrayed by the chromatic fragment first heard in the English horn at 66, which gives an effect of incredible ugliness here in dissonance against the simple but graceful waltz tune.

The remainder of the tableau is narrative. The waltz breaks off abruptly as the two discover the jealous Petrushka at the door; bits of his triadic theme are heard after 76, first in muted trumpet and cornet, then in the other brass, followed by several measures of an angry outburst from the Moor. The two rivals scuffle at 78, as the Ballerina faints, but Petrushka is no match for his much larger and stronger opponent and is tossed through the door. There is no semblance of melody in this section, merely a rushing flurry of scale figures and arpeggios clustered in sharp dissonance leading to violent reiterated chords at 81 as the lights go down on the angry but victorious Moor.

The third and fourth tableaux are connected by the same off-stage drumming that Stravinsky uses to link the other scenes. The action in this last tableau takes place again in the square, towards

6. The melody for Stravinsky's A section is taken from Lanner's *Steyrische Tänze*, Opus 165, and the second one is borrowed from the first waltz in *Die Schönbrunner*, Opus 200. Lanner's original pieces may be found in Volume 65 of the *Denkmäler der Tonkunst in Österreich*, pp. 78 f. and 107 f., as edited by Alfred Orel.

evening, with the festivities approaching their peak. The gaiety of the crowd is depicted in the restless, shimmering, brilliantly orchestrated introduction (82–88), which works up to a climax as the curtain goes up at 88, then subsides to curious undulating, accordion-like chords in the winds and brass leading to the first set dance of the tableau.

The core of the tableau consists of a succession of dances, each in some simple form, performed by groups who form part of the street celebration. First there is a dance of a group of nursemaids, beginning at 90. The principal melody, a Russian folk song "Ia vechor moloda," is introduced in fragmentary form in the oboes and horns, then is given out in its four-measure entirety by first violins and horns at 92, against fragments of material from the first tableau played by the flutes. After several repetitions, a transitional section at 95 leads to a second tune at 96; this too is a Russian folk tune, "Akh vy sieni, moi sieni," played first by the oboes, then clarinets, trumpets, and finally full orchestra. This first dance is brought to a climax as these two tunes are played against one another in counterpart (98–100), the first by the violins and winds and the second by the brass.

Next a peasant enters, leading a bear, and the crowd watches as he plays on the pipes (solo clarinet in the orchestra) while the bear walks on his hind legs (solo tuba), at 100. After this brief interlude there it a bit of general crowd dancing again (101) to some of the same music that opened the tableau.

A drunken merchant appears (102), amusing himself by tossing banknotes to the crowd. He dances to a sturdy diatonic tune played by unison strings; the scrambling of the crowd is suggested by the winds and brass, which continue the agitated figurations of the previous section. Two gypsies who have accompanied him dance, at 103, to a simple, four-measure, triadic tune. The merchant's melody comes back at 105, followed by the gypsy music again at 106 and 107, as the three leave the stage. Thus the section is cast in a simple ABAB form.

A dance of coachmen and grooms follows, based on another Russian folk tune, "Ia na gorkku shla." Characteristically, Stravinsky first sets a rhythmic accompaniment in motion (108), sets fragments of his tune against this (108–110), then offers the tune in its entirety at 111. The nursemaids return, as the orchestra plays "Ia vechor moloda" again at 112, and this section is brought to a noisy climax (114–116) with the return of the coachmen's tune, scored this time for full orchestra.

Now various maskers dance, each with appropriate music. A first group frolics at 117; at 118, a devil taunts the crowd; two comic characters, dressed as a goat and a pig, engage in brief byplay at 120; another group dances at 121, to music reminiscent of the 5/8 section of the first tableau; the entire crowd joins in general dancing at 122. All this takes place to music in which interest is mostly rhythmic, with only bits and fragments of melody, a succession of brief sections that fall into no larger formal shape, and which lead to a loud and almost frenzied climax after 124.

A scream is heard from the puppet theater (125), Petrushka's scream, in the trumpets, and the crowd abruptly stops its revelry. From here to the end the action on stage is narrative, with music serving to underline the tragic pantomime that unfolds. Petrushka rushes into the square, pursued by the Moor, who breaks away from the Ballerina's attempts to restrain him. Furious, rushing chromatic passages depict the Moor's rage (before and after 128), and there is a vicious thud from the orchestra as he strikes down Petrushka with his saber. The stunned crowd gathers around the corpse of the puppet (129), as harmonics and tremolos in the strings support lamenting fragments in the winds. The Magician arrives, to a few march-like measures in the lowest winds (130), and an echo of his music from the first tableau is heard as he views the puppet's body. The crowd disperses, to undulating chords in the horns, and the Magician drags the corpse towards the puppet theater (131). At 132, Petrushka's triadic motive, played on a small muted trumpet, cuts through the sound of the horns, and the puppet's ghost is seen over the little theater, thumbing his nose at the Magician. The latter drops the corpse and hurries off, looking fearfully over his shoulder. Petrushka's motive is heard one last time, the undulating figure (which Berg must surely have had in mind when composing the very end of *Wozzeck*) returns for two more measures, and the drama ends with its famous cadence making a final reference to the C-F♯ relationship that has permeated so much of the work.

To recapitulate briefly, *Petrushka* can best be understood today as it was fifty years ago, as a dramatic work in which the musical organization is determined in large part by the stage action, which in turn is often effective precisely because the accompanying music is so beautifully conceived, worked out, and orchestrated. The score can stand alone, as a concert piece, and is best known today in this form; but it is only on those rare occasions when the ballet is mounted that one can fully understand and appreciate what a work of genius it is.

The score resists analysis by methods that can tell us so much about a Machaut motet, a Beethoven quartet, or a Webern symphony, but it is a piece with remarkable unity, despite the immense variety of harmonic and melodic ingredients. Stravinsky's most characteristic techniques in *Petrushka* are the use of this wide range of material, the alternation of simple dances with open forms that accompany pantomime on the stage, the juxtaposition of simple folk and popular songs with sections of music in which there are no discernible melodic lines, the introduction of a melody in fragments before it is heard in its entirety, and the non-systematic use of similar musical material in different sections of the work.

Stravinsky has said of the work, *"Petroushka,* like *The Firebird* and *Le Sacre du printemps,* has already survived a half-century of destructive popularity, and if it does not sound as fresh today as, for example, Schoenberg's *Five Pieces for Orchestra* and Webern's six, the reason is partly that the Viennese pieces have been protected by fifty years of neglect." [7] But the piece has retained its vitality as few pieces do. It is as fresh as ever to each new generation, and if it is true that some of the freshness has worn off for older listeners, it has been replaced by the sort of affection that one develops for only too few compositions in the standard repertory.

7. Stravinsky, *Expositions and Developments,* p. 156.

ESSAYS, VIEWS, AND COMMENTS

Unless specified otherwise, all numbered footnotes in the following essays are those of the author. References in the essays to places in the score have been bracketed and changed to refer to this edition.

EDITH SITWELL

The Russian Ballet in England †

As this appreciation by the poetess Edith Sitwell shows, the tragic puppet
Petrushka became a hero for English intellectuals, who took him to heart
even more than the French.

Before the arrival of the first company of the Russian ballet in England, the average person had never dreamt that movement could
convey a philosophy of life as complete and rounded as any world could
be. We had been galvanised by the vitality of the music-hall stage, but
this is often a mechanical life, animating a slightly masked world; or
rather, let us say, it is not so much life itself as a distorting mirror of
life, in which we see our faces and our natures broadened into a grin—
sometimes merely sardonic, sometimes tragic. For underneath the dis-
torted good-humour of the "turns," heaven knows what bitter hatred
may not hide itself. Laughter itself seems mechanical as a switchback;
it swings from a height to unutterable depths, and it has the same inevit-
able movement as the switchback. And the rouge on the laughing masks
is, from time to time, not a little like blood. Thus, under the violent
rays of a many-coloured sun, that dissects our hypocrisies bone from
bone, we move somnambulantly through this mirror-bright world, and
cling into some mournful patterning; while the harsh mordant music
strips off our flesh and shows us, marionettes that we are, clothed only
in our primal lust.

    Then came the Russian ballet, and with it, our clearer philosophy.
These movements, and the bright shrilling of the colour which is part of
their speech, are an interpretation, not of a mood alone, but often of
life itself. Seen with the clearness of a dream, these bright magical movements have, now the intense vitality of the heart of life, now the rigidity
of death; and for speech they have the more universal and larger language
of music, interpreting still more clearly these strange beings whose life is

† From Edith Sitwell, *Russian Ballet Gift Book*, London, 1921, pp. 7–14.

so intense, yet to whom living, seen from the outside, is but a brief and tragic happiness upon the greenest grass, in some unknown flashing summer weather. "Dames qui tournoient sur les terrasses voisines de la mer, enfantes et géantes, superbes noires dans la mousse vert-de-gris, bijoux debouts sur le sol gras des bosquets et des jardinets dégélés, jeunes mères et sœurs aux regards pleins de pélérinages, sultanes, princesses de démarche et de costume tyranniques, petites étrangères et personnes doucement malheureuses,"[1] all these pass before our eyes, sometimes building sand-castles upon the shores of eternity, sometimes chasing the music like butterflies in the ephemeral life of the stage. For indeed, their tragedies seem but as the tragedy of two painted butterflies who, intent upon their play, have floated all unawares into the courts of Hell. Strange eyes may stare at them, "simian faces, green flowers streaked with encre de chine," look askance at them, chattering in an unknown tongue; they may float through those jewelled green gardens for ever—but they scarcely care, and we care not at all. Life is so ephemeral. Their tragedies pierce us, yet leave no scar, for we understand them only as children understand; we are protected by our own individuality—so unalterably different from theirs; and all the while we are as remote from the world in which these alien beings move as are the children dressed in mourning of whom Arthur Rimbaud writes in his prose poem, "Après le Deluge": like these, "from our great glass house we look at the marvellous pictures." So we sit, in the loneliness of identity, watching the movements growing and ripening like fruit, or curling with the fantastic inevitability of waves seen by a Chinese painter; and thought is never absent from these ballets. In Petrouchka we see mirrored for us, in these clear sharp outlines and movements, all the philosophy of Laforgue,[2] as the puppets move somnambulantly through the dark of our hearts. For this ballet, alone among them all,

---

1. This passage is from Arthur Rimbaud's prose poem "Enfance" ("Childhood"), the second of the famous *Illuminations,* published for the first time in 1886 in five issues of the Symbolist periodical *La Vogue.* It may be translated: "Women who wander on terraces by the sea; small girls and giantesses; superb blacks in the verdigris moss, jewels standing on the rich ground of thickets and little thawed gardens, young mothers and sisters with glances full of pilgrimages, sultanas, princesses of tyrannical costume and bearing, little foreign girls and young ladies gently unhappy." [*Editor*]

2. Jules Laforgue (1860–1887) was a French symbolist poet. His major works include five volumes of poetry, published between 1885 and 1894, three volumes of prose writings (including *Moralités légendaires,* published in Paris in 1887), and a translation into French of some of the works of Walt Whitman. [*Editor*]

shatters our glass house about our ears and leaves us terrified, haunted by its tragedy. The music, harsh, crackling rags of laughter, shrieks at us like some brightly-painted Punch and Judy show, upon grass as shrill as anger, as dulled at hate. Sometimes it jangles thin as the wires on which these half-human puppets move; or a little hurdy-gurdy valse sounds hollow, with the emptiness of the hearts of the passing people, "vivant de can-cans de clochers, disant: 'Quel temps fera-t-il demain,' 'Voici l'hiver qui vient,' 'Nous n'avons pas eu de prunes cette année.' " [3] But sometimes the music has terrible moments of darkness, as when the Magician gropes in the booth for his puppet Petrouchka. And there is one short march, quick and terrible, in which the drum-taps are nothing but the anguished beat of the clown's heart as he makes his endless battle against materialism. And we know that we are watching our own tragedy. Do we not all know that little room at the back of our poor clown's booth —that little room with the hopeful tinsel stars and the badly-painted ancestral portrait of God? Have we not all battered our heads through the flimsy paper walls—only to find blackness? In the dead Petrouchka, we know that it is our own poor wisp of soul that is weeping so pitifully to us from the top of the booth, outside life for ever, with no one to warm him or comfort him, while the bright-coloured rags that were the clown's body lie, stabbed to the heart, in the mire of the street—and, with Claudius, we cry out for "Lights, lights, more lights." [4]

3. This quotation from Laforgue's *Moralités légendaires* (Legendary Moralities) may be translated: "Living with can-cans of clocks, saying: 'What time will it be tomorrow,' 'It is winter that is coming,' 'We have had no prunes this year.' " [*Editor*]

4. The reference is to the Players' Scene (Act III, Scene 2) in Shakespeare's *Hamlet*. [*Editor*]

CYRIL W. BEAUMONT

[*Petrushka in London*] †

This passage by the English ballet critic Cyril W. Beaumont is perhaps the
finest description ever written of the visual and dramatic effect of the ballet, and of the performances of the principal dancers who created the main
roles.

Every ballet-goer knows that the three puppets are supported from
the shoulders by an iron stand set at the back of each cell, which
enables the puppets to execute the curious mechanical dance with which
the first scene draws to a close. Nijinsky's dancing was unusual. When
the Showman gave the signal for the puppets to dance, Nijinsky succeeded in investing the movements of his legs with a looseness sug-
gesting that foot, leg, and thigh were threaded on a string attached to
the hip; there was a curiously fitful quality in his movements, his limbs
spasmodically leapt or twisted or stamped like the reflex actions of limbs
whose muscles have been subjected to an electric current.

The whole production of the ballet was inspired. There was the
blackout which brought the first scene to an abrupt conclusion, and the
roll of drums that symbolised the passing crowd of sightseers outside the
booth, and at the same time held the attention of the theatre audience,
while the drop-curtain was lowered to permit of each change of scene,
and then raised to disclose it.

There were four scenes, the first and last being the same, the scene of
the fair; the other two showed Petrouchka's cell and the Moor's cell
respectively. The second and third scenes were small ones set inside the
main one, and since, in these, there were never more than three characters at one time, the contrasting gaiety of the outdoor scene with the
comparative quiet of the indoor cells in which the puppets lived, was
most effectively suggested.

---

† From Cyril W. Beaumont, *The Diaghilev Ballet in London*, London, 1940, pp.
43–50. Reprinted by permission of the author.

The second scene, Petrouchka's cell, was the most unusual from the musical aspect, and at the first performance the members of the audience were considerably disconcerted by the piercing shrieks which conveyed Petrouchka's unhappiness. It was only gradually that it was seen how exactly right were those strident shrieks.

Nijinsky as Petrouchka dominated this and the last scene. He wore a thick white cotton blouse with a frilled collar edged with red, a red tie, satin trousers chequered in crimson and yellow, blue boots of soft leather, and a red and white hat with a tassel.

His features were made up a kind of putty colour, presumably a suggestion of wood; his nose was built up to have a thicker base; his eyebrows were painted out and replaced by a wavy line set half an inch higher; his lips were compressed together; his eyes seemed devoid of lid and socket, and suggested a pair of boot-buttons or two blobs of black paint; there was a little red on his cheeks. His features were formed into a sad and unhappy mask, an expression which remained constant throughout the ballet.

I have seen no one approach Nijinsky's rendering of Petrouchka, for, as I have said elsewhere, he suggested a puppet that sometimes aped a human being, whereas all the other interpreters conveyed a dancer imitating a puppet. He seemed to have probed the very soul of the character with astonishing intuition. Did he, in one of his dark moods of introspection, feel conscious of a strange parallel between Petrouchka and himself, and the Showman and Diaghilev?

Despite his set features he was, paradoxically enough, most expressive, his emotions being conveyed by the movements of his arms, the tilt of his head, and the various angles at which he bent his body from the waist. In general, his arms were stiff and extended like the arms of a puppet pivoted at the shoulder, but their meaning was plain. I well remember his dramatic entrance in the second scene when the double door leading to his cell burst open and he was propelled through it by the Showman's cruel boot. As if in acute pain, he tottered forward on his toes, flung up his arms, and threw back his head.

How vividly he presented his despair, his unhappiness, his misery, as he fingered and plucked at his clothes, the symbol of his servitude. Then he sank on his knees, and, with his stiff arms, now bent at the elbow, struck his neck first on one side and then on the other in a state of utter dejection at his pitiful lot.

Suddenly the folding door burst open and the Dancer appeared, to give him new hope. How excitedly he jerked his arms in greeting! But alas, the Dancer resented his strange manner of courtship and slammed the door in his face. Imagine his sorrow at this new affront. In a frenzy of rage and despair, he sought to escape from his cell and follow her.

Now I want to emphasize that this scene does not consist merely of kneeling at the bottom of the double door, making pattering movements of the hands up the wall and tearing at it until an opening is forced, through which Petrouchka's head and arms disappear, while his body remains within the room. To obtain the full dramatic value of this episode, the dancer must induce within himself a state of emotion such as a puppet temporarily endowed with life might feel under like circumstances, and then express it in terms of the movements designed by the choreographer. In most of the presentations of this scene I have been conscious of a certain casual approach, a sort of "now I do the business of pattering on the wall and bring the scene to a close." In short, you had a feeling that the movements were done because they had been prescribed, and less with the realisation that they were the expression of a sudden mad moment of revolt on Petrouchka's part against the conditions which, when he was not performing to the public, reduced him to the status of a prisoner, confined within the narrow limits of his dark room.

Nijinsky gave an impressive performance of this episode. The Dancer's departure left him stunned for a brief moment, then he made you aware, through the almost imperceptible shaking of his head and body, and the twitching of his limbs, of the tumult of emotions stirring within him. Suddenly he flung himself on his knees by the doors, his gloved hands gliding ceaselessly up and down the jamb, higher and higher, as he tried to find an opening. Gradually he rose to his feet, still fingering the jamb more and more feverishly as his sense of frustration grew. Abruptly he rejected the door and passed his hands over the wall, faster and faster, while his head and limbs continually twitched from the intensity of his eagerness to escape. All at once his groping fingers found a weak spot and tore the paper apart—a piercing scream of triumph burst from the orchestra as his head and shoulders fell through the gap. His body went limp, curved in an inverted "v," as if he had fainted from exhaustion, while his arms, dropped in a vertical line, swung idly to and fro, as if still quivering from the violence of his efforts.

Another great moment occurred in the final scene when Petrouchka, struck by a blow from the Moor's scimitar, collapsed and sank on the snow-covered ground. He went inert like a broken doll. It was only with the greatest difficulty that he was able to raise himself from the ground. His head lolled to and fro as though attached to his neck by a piece of string. His arms jerked feebly. The green glare of a Bengal light turned his features a ghastly green. Then he fell back and rolled over on to his side.

Nijinsky's performance made a great impression upon me. As in all his creations, he absorbed himself completely in the character presented. His conceptions were illumined by genius; they were vital and memorable; and in the parts which he created he set a standard which his successors in those roles have never approached, let alone equalled.

Karsavina looked charming as the Dancer in her lace-fringed pantalettes, striped dull red and maroon, her pale mauve skirt, and her crimson velvet bodice with white sleeves trimmed with gold bands. Her hair, dressed in the short ringlets which became her so well, was crowned with a crimson velvet toque, trimmed with white fur. Her make-up was flesh-pink with a bright dab of red on each cheek. Her eyes were given an air of exaggerated surprise by short black lines painted ray-like about them.

She made the Dancer an impressionable, flighty young woman, and all her movements had a crispness and tautness which gave them a most attractively piquant quality. Her little dance with the trumpet was admirably timed and as gay and as sprightly as could be. Her daintiness made an excellent foil for the agitated, twitching, hypersensitive Petrouchka and the vain, lumbering, brutish Moor.

One of the most vivid of my recollections of Karsavina in this role is associated with the third scene, where she is captivated by the overwhelming personality of the Moor, so splendid a figure in his suit of emerald green and silver. When the Dancer paid him a visit, he dropped the cocoanut with which he had been playing, and, plumping himself on the divan, brazenly seized the Dancer and pulled her on to his knees. How delightfully she suggested by the particular tilting of her head and shoulders the nervous thrill she experienced from that bold attack. But when Petrouchka most inconsiderately burst upon the lovers and squeaked his indignation, her innate modesty returned and she quickly jumped to her feet, jerking up her hands to hide her burning cheeks.

Orlov created the role of the Moor when Petrouchka was first performed—at Paris; unfortunately, I never saw him. But Kotchetovsky, who played the Moor in the London *première*, has remained for me the best interpreter of that part, although Bolm ran him closely. Kotchetovsky made the Moor a big, burly, clumsy fellow, childishly vain of his physical strength and his imposing uniform. He made him a good-humoured lout with a child-like propensity for showing-off at the slightest provocation, yet he did the simplest movements with such a smacking of his thick lips, such rolling of eyeballs, such gusto, that you could not help sharing in his extravagant delight.

And I must not forget Cecchetti as the old Showman, a mysterious, enigmatic figure, his every movement timed to perfection. How calmly and carelessly he followed the policeman come to acquaint him of the murder of Petrouchka, an absurd notion he quickly disposed of by his contemptuous shaking of the limp figure to prove that Petrouchka was nothing more than wood and sawdust. Then came the dramatic moment when, as he strolled homewards, dragging the puppet's limp body behind him, preparatory to returning it to its cell, there was a succession of eerie squeaks and Petrouchka's ghost appeared at the top of the booth, to mock his master, who, shaken and terrified by this unexpected and inexplicable phenomenon, hastily took to flight.

I can still see the abrupt end of Cecchetti's leisurely walk as he jerked back on his heels, his whole body tensed in an attitude of listening. Then, as Petrouchka's mocking squeaks were repeated, there flashed over Cecchetti's features a look of mingled bewilderment and surprise, which swiftly changed to abject fear. Full of apprehension, he half-turned his head in the direction of the sound, and, as he caught sight of the roof of the booth with the head and shoulders of that ghostly figure gibbering with its stiff arms, a chill sweat broke out on his forehead. He smoothed his brow with his trembling hand, shaking so violently that his hat fell from his head. The sound of that object striking the ground startled him into immediate action, and, filled with a frenzied desire to escape, he scurried away, as fast as his trembling legs would carry him.

H. T. PARKER

~~~~~~~~~~~~~

[*Petrushka in Boston*] †

American critics acquitted themselves extremely well in their first en-
counters with *Petrushka*. It must be remembered that it, and *The Firebird,*
were the first major works by Stravinsky played in this country, and the musical style of these works came as a greater surprise to audiences and critics
on this side of the Atlantic because of lesser familiarity with important music of the decade before. Despite this, many of the American reviews were
quite perceptive and sympathetic.

Thus, "Pétrouchka" mimed and danced for the second time in Boston last evening, conveys so much to so many a faculty that it is
hard to isolate the impression of Stravinsky's music from the swarming
sensations of the whole. Obviously, it is music written with wholly
delineative and enforcing purpose. The sounds of a folk-fair, like that
which fills the stage in the first and final scenes of the ballet, are bound
to be hard, rough and discordant and Stravinsky shapes the matter and
the manner of his music so that it shall bear them unmitigated, and even
enhanced, to his watching hearers. If two hurdy-gurdies are playing in
rivalry, as they are quite likely to do in such a place and time, then
shall the orchestra sound with their jangling voices in trumpery tunes.
The dances that the folk dance are sure to be stoutly rhythmed and rude-
voiced and so the brass-choir beats out the rhythm and blares out the
tune until the whole stage, the whole auditorium and every step on the
one and every ear in the other ring with them. When the Ballerina dances
for her beloved Blackmoor, tootling upon her toy trumpet meanwhile,
there is just one sort of tune that suits in such a situation such an empty-
headed little automaton of a puppet show, viz., the cheap and common
tune of ballet music at its lowest terms that the cornets of the orchestra
smirk out again and again.

Scarcely a detail of the action on the stage escapes Stravinsky. A

† From the *Boston Evening Transcript*, February 8, 1916.

newcomer to the fair leads a dancing bear across the scene and for the moment the orchestra lumbers and grunts with the passage of the clumsy beast. Yet all this is not merely the fortuitous and expert delineation of externals. Stravinsky's imagination runs much deeper and finer. Piteous little Pétrouchka returns to his box, his spirit riven with the impotent love for the disdainful Ballerina. He tortures himself with his grief and longing; he beats himself against the barriers of fate; he imagines himself wooing and winning her, and in the next instant feels the futility in this relentless world of all the little ruses with which he would beguile her; of all the little charms that he would display before her; of even the great affection that moves him to such vanities. He flings his little puppet-body about the box; he beats the air with his puppet-arms and legs; he contorts his blank puppet-face with whatever mood or impulse is for the instant upon him. While Mr. Massin [sic], miming Pé-trouchka, is projecting all these things upon the spectator's eye, so Stravinsky's music is projecting them upon his ear until the two imparting means bring irresistible illusion. Thus the spectator knows and feels only Pétrouchka's emotions. Yet as the eye simultaneously sees his puppet-like contortions, so the music both mirrors these motions and bears the passions within of which they are the futile and comic expression. It is music of outward shows and inner moods; it is music of grotesquerie, and it is music of tragedy.

As it should, the purpose of this music has altogether conditioned Stravinsky's procedure with it. If keys must jangle to gain the delineation or the enforcing suggestion that he seeks, jangle they do. If for like end progression or modulation must rasp the ear, Stravinsky lets it rasp it, mindful that at the same time it is enkindling the listening imagination to illusion. If vivid suggestion engenders strange juxtaposition of chords, side by side, none the less, they go. If timbre must be superposed on timbre to gain such an illusion of a particular sound as that of two hand organs, Stravinsky superposes them accordingly. If his characterizing purpose as in this and that scene of Pétrouchka himself, can be best accomplished by the voice of a piano, then that instrument is not only joined to the orchestra but the other instruments are made subordinate to it or even silent beside it. In all this procedure Stravinsky seeks and gains the exact sensation that he would convey to his audience. He does not spare and he does not waste a note in the process. The imagined end stands clear; the applied means, used with equal imagination, accomplish it and straightway he goes forward briefly, directly.

The wonder of this music is similarly two-fold. On the one side is the wealth of delineative and characterizing imagination that can so transmute into tones and individualize there every essential personage, every essential incident, and every outstanding quality in "Pétrouchka" conceived as mimed and danced drama and picture; that can fasten upon every salient detail in all three and embody it in the music; that can summon and maintain the illusion of a puppet tragedy in all its grotesque externals and all its inner ironies. On the other stands the imagination in resources and in the application of them that makes Stravinsky such a master of rhythms and timbres as music even in this fortunate day hardly knows, and that makes him hardly less a master of all the other delineative and characterizing means of present music. Whatever he will seems ready at its call. Melody in the conventional sense, as in "L'Oiseau de Feu" or his opera of "Le Rossignol," as yet unknown in performance in America, answers as readily as do the biting chords or the piercing timbres of this or that passage in "Pétrouchka." He can write music of a wondrous, sensuous richness and beauty, as in "L'Oiseau de Feu"; and he can write music that is all astringent suggestion and penetration as he has in "Pétrouchka." In both he can write music that is as marvellously lucid, direct, and economical in the chosen tonal speech; music that may sound thin to ears long accustomed to a lush, harmonic, and instrumental procedure, but that in very thinness has a new intensity and precision of voice.

Above all, this two-fold imagination may have given him the courage —no less precious and no less essential—to write in his own way for his own ends; to let his intent condition his form and procedure, as he quietly ignored the conventions and devised his own expressive means after his own fashion to achieve to the full the taste he had set before him.

Whatever else the Russian Ballet has done in Boston, it has made known to it, as none but it could do since Stravinsky writes now almost wholly for the stage, the remarkable music of one of the most illustrious composers of our time and in true and vivid image.

WALLACE FOWLIE

Petrouchka's Wake †

I

Only a straw-stuffed puppet, this modern hero! His soul is so tiny that we might almost say he has no soul at all. The flat bright colors of his costumes are the simple basic passions which he has learned by rote and which he typifies under the white grease paint. But his mouth is human in its tortured line and his eyes have at times the light of all of man's prayers and loves. Human in his final convulsions and in his death, he appears only as a caricature of man in his life, an hallucinated clown whose jerkiness and animation depict the comic of passions. The crowd must forget the tragedy of passions. He is the will of the crowd. He is the tawdry projection of the crowd's willful flight from reality. He is the soul of the crowd when it has no courage and no heroism. Petrouchka is the reminiscence of what was human.

Yet the passion of all past heroes is in the puppet. Petrouchka is in love. Within the sawdust of his awkward body, there is a grain of life which has all the swelling recklessness and all the trembling blindness of Antony and Othello. Love can change a man into a clown and change a clown into a man. Modern literature no longer contemplates the great principle of love in a hero of stature and vigor. As though he were engaged in some laboratory experiment, the creative artist has grafted the principle of love on innocent and helpless replicas of man. Petrouchka's white face against the blank walls of his cell shows up clearly. Art is an experiment taking place under a steady flood light. The hero-clown is exhibited, even in his cell and in his solitude, and appears as visible as if he were tied on an operating table. The greatness of his figure has vanished, but the unity of his being is still the same. The divine in him,

† From *Essays in Honor of Albert Feuillerat*, edited by Henry Peyre, *Yale Romantic Studies*, XXII (1943), 249–53. Reprinted by permission of the publisher, Yale University Press.

which is the force of his love, beats against the sawdust walls of his limp body, as he beats against the fictitious cardboard walls of his cell. For there is no greatness, no dignity in his world: the planks he parades on are barely nailed together and the rope which pulls the faded stage curtain seems to break at each night stand. Integrated, pure, tragic, his love for the insipid ballerina dominates the show, melts the grease paint, releases his spirit in its dance before the ideal.

II

For Plato, a man's love is his search for himself. Without much juggling of terms, this definition can apply to divine love because the self which is sought is that pure part of being, between which being and God there is no obstacle. The clown traffics with the childlike part of himself. When a child desires an object, no amount of reasoning or logic can change him from his desire. Pierrot, Pinocchio, Petrouchka belong to the race of children who die before their desire is realized. Their fate is a mock tragedy because they have no sense of shame at their plight. Children and clowns never realize that their plight is universal and shared: they are the innocent scapegoats of all the adult and bourgeois spectators who watch half-amused, half-puzzled, in the antics and incarnations of the clown and the child the projection of their own undivulged desires.

And so, love in the puppet, as does love in the prophet, who is still another specimen of the abandoned scapegoat, grows into tragic intensity. Petrouchka's love is the pure symbol of tragedy: rapid, powerful, crushing. His first movements are as futile as the first words of Phèdre. He is already, at the beginning of each performance, in the domain of death. His daily ritual is a flight from a vocation of mimicry and humor into a personal experience of love. There he lives as he had never lived in his showman's trade, and there he dies because of his infidelity to the lesser life.

The contemporary painters realized the clown's tragedy and its depiction of the hero. As all women were in the painted Virgin of the Italian Renaissance, so all men are in the painted clown of modern France. Cézanne, Rouault, Picasso have re-created all the poses of Petrouchka. He lives also in the *Pitre Châtié* of Mallarmé and in the *Orphée* of Cocteau. As in the ballet of Stravinsky and Fokine, Mallarmé's clown makes a hole in his tent and escapes into the world of love where he is struck down with a bolt from heaven. Petrouchka is related to the chil-

dren of the sun and the race of **Phèdre** because his love consumes him in
its frenzy. If Phèdre has beauty and grace, her desire is depicted as mon-
strous and grotesque; but the very purity of Petrouchka's desire is de-
formed by his unnatural body and the exaggerated traits of his counte-
nance.

III

Modern poetry is a world familiar with the spiritual struggle of Petrouchka. In fact, the poet at all times is not unlike the clown. He is the
type of man to whom the French word "chétif" [1] applies. When the poet
is not performing as poet, it may well be that he is collapsing or dying
somewhere. Mallarmé's faun is comparable to the poet whose experience
is never realized, whose experience is never joy. In Hart Crane's *Southern
Cross*, the chétif poet wants the "nameless Woman of the South": his
tragedy is that of loving what is impossible and unreal, as Petrouchka's is
that of loving what is inferior and unresponsive. The theme of innocency
and "childhood havens" in Ben Belitt's verse is a statement not of love or
tragedy, but of spiritual fervor akin with Petrouchka's fervor and "faint
heart" and abiding oneness. In the recently published *Lincoln Lyrics* of
John Malcolm Brinnin, we read a poet struck with the choreographic
gauntness and "graceless strength" of a hero possessing none of the traditional heroic glamor. The space and site of Lincoln's childhood were not
epic-marked, but "acorn-punctuated." His love was a "Song of Songs on
Illinois."

The contemporary poet, if he is not Petrouchka himself, sees what is
tragic and eternal in Petrouchka. If the poet is not inhabiting the very
heart of despair, as Petrouchka and Hart Crane were, he is concerned
with the preparation for that despair which he discovers in what Saint
Augustine would have called the world of his universal memory. In a
spiritual sense, then, the poet is the clown either because of the total and
hysteric absorption of himself in the object loved, or because of his wait-
ing in the mythic part of a world which the rest of the world contemplates
with feelings of recognition and amusement and remoteness.

Characters in prose fiction, and some of the most striking in recent
times, bear traits of Petrouchka and traces of his agony. In Flaubert's *Un
Cœur Simple*, Félicité is a counterpart of the puppet. She loved instinctively and without hope the persons nearest to her until they all died and

---

1. The literal meaning of "chétif" is pitiful, worthless, or puny. [*Editor*]

she was left with the symbol of frustration: the stuffed parrot. In this caricature of affection, both hideous and pathetic, there is the enactment of a clown's strategy. When Petrouchka is killed by the Moor's scimitar, his body turns out to be only a straw-stuffed figure, and when Félicité is dying, her ultimate vision of reality is the wide-spread wings of her parrot mounting heavenward. These are the heroes who loved what didn't exist and who died embracing the air.

Such frustration as Félicité's is not reserved solely for the simple in heart. Aschenbach, in Thomas Mann's *Death in Venice,* is the intellectual and artist whose insensate love for the young boy Tadzio has in it the same mockery and unreality as Petrouchka's love has. A great human passion lodged in a puppet's body is as tragic as the love of a mature artist for a young boy to whom he can never speak. Both are tragic because of their ludicrous unreality. The puppet, the servant girl, and the artist represent three levels of existence in which the same tragedy of disproportion occurs. Petrouchka's dance and rhythmic contortions, Félicité's stuffed parrot, which is a kind of relic of her dead love, and Aschenbach's fever-infested Venice where he continues to live with Tadzio and death until his real death comes, are the symbols of what has happened to each one; and in each case, it is the symbol of the irremediable.

Even in stories published last year, Petrouchka's ghost continues to dictate to his new children the awkward passion of loneliness. *A Memory* in Eudora Welty's book, *A Curtain of Green,* with the delicacy and suggestiveness of a woman's skill in writing, recalls the incident in a young girl's life of a certain morning when she touched her friend's wrist as they passed on the stairs in school. Later, on a beach where she is watching the crude playfulness of a family, she tries to live in her memory of love and in all its pitiful singleness of gesture. The man in the family group pours sand inside his wife's bathing suit between her breasts, and when she stands up "the lumps of mashed and folded sand came emptying out . . . as though her breasts themselves had turned to sand." The image has the same mixture of horror and grotesqueness and comedy as Petrouchka's dance; and there is the same unreality of the exterior world and the acute prolonged reality of the timid heart.

V

Petrouchka's wake is attended by a vast company. The modern artist has seized upon the dual body of the puppet: the limp straw body stretched out on the market place, and the writhing body of the spirit as it appears over the tent at the end of the ballet. He has recast the dualism of Greek and Judeo-Christian philosophy in the quiescent deathlike Petrouchka and the violent energizing Petrouchka. The ancient problem of appearance and reality is the rapid life story of the puppet. His garb is the clown's and his grease paint is the performer's, but his destiny is suffering and death.

The greatest of all Petrouchkas is James Joyce's Earwicker.[2] Flaccid and melting, half conscious and half asleep, H. C. Earwicker, who is the comic and the tragic of all men, both participates in and watches a long procession of eidolons. Shadows of himself and of all men parade in cinematographic ease through his sleeplessness. Their focal point is love and the nightly seizure of passion. Earwicker lies beside his wife in bed, but a world of time and change is between them. His mind moves out of his body, as Petrouchka's spirit abandoned his punctured straw corpse, and wanders to another bed where his sons sleep. The old man is the young man; the puppet is the lover; the prince is the pumpkin: "I thought you were all glittering with the noblest of carriage. You're only a bumpkin."

The first ballet on the program might easily be *Giselle:* classic, simple, natural, where the hero loves the heroine and she loves him. But *Petrouchka,* which ends the program, is the modern distortion. The tragedy of *Giselle* is a fairy story and the fairy story of *Petrouchka* is a tragedy.

---

2. Humphrey Chimpden Earwicker is a character in Joyce's *Finnegan's Wake.* A tavern-keeper in Chapelizod (a suburb of Dublin), he, with his wife, twin sons, and daughter, is one of the fixed points around which the events and other characters of the novel revolve. [*Editor*]

FREDERICK W. STERNFELD

Some Russian Folk Songs
in Stravinsky's Petrouchka †

In his memoirs [1] Eduard Strauss, writing of the origins of Joseph Lanner's waltz tunes, raises the age-old question of melodic originality. Did the popularity of Lanner's waltzes ultimately obscure their actual origin so that they became popular themes of apparently anonymous authorship or did Lanner, having first made their acquaintance in the street and countryside, then turn the melodies into waltz tunes of his own? Strauss does not attempt an answer other than to defend, in a general way, Lanner's originality (as well as that of Johann Strauss) against those critics who accused them of appropriating Viennese street tunes, as though thematic originality were of value in itself. One could pursue this line of thought back to the beginnings of musical history, and it is to be hoped that at least one critic may, in turn, have asked Strauss why a waltz deserved a loftier origin than many a Lutheran chorale of humble secular birth. Appositely enough, the Lanner tune with which Eduard Strauss illustrates his question occurs in the Third Picture of *Petrouchka* along with another Lanner waltz taken from the *Steyerische Tänze*.[2]

† From *Music Library Association Notes*, II (1945), 98–104. Reprinted by permission. Some footnotes, and the appendix listing various folksong collections, have been omitted; measure numbers have been changed for more convenient references to the present score. [*Editor*]

In addition to the persons mentioned in the body of the article, I want to express my gratitude for the assistance I have received from the staffs of the Yale University Library, the New York Public Library, and the Library of Congress; also to Mr. Bruce Simonds of the Yale School of Music and to Mr. Joseph Yasser of New York. [*Author*]

1. *Erinnerungen*, Leipzig and Wien, Franz Deuticke, 1906, pp. 168–170.

2. Lanner's *Die Schönbrunner*, Op. 200 (1842), p. 107, and *Steyrische Tänze*, Op. 165 (1840), p. 78, edited by Alfred Orel, in vol. 65 of the *Denkmäler der Tonkunst in Österreich*, are introduced in the Third Picture [i.e. Tableau] of *Petrouchka* [at 72, and at 5 measures after 71, respectively].

Und der Lan - ner   war gleich a - ner,   sprach ge - sel - lig

Whatever their origin, Lanner's waltzes have taken their place in *Petrouchka* in a cosmopolitan company, for the palette on which Stravinsky mixes his colors for this Carnival scene in St. Petersburg's Admiralty Square in the 1830s is rich and varied: beside these Austrian dances of the same period, we find a French music hall ditty of the early 1900s (*Elle avait un' jambe en bois*)[3] and, to come finally to the subject of our article, traditional Russian folk songs of no particular period. Unlike the Lanner waltzes of debatable origin, certain portions of the thematic material in *Petrouchka* can be specifically traced to five native folk songs which are available in the collections of Rimsky-Korsakov, Tchaikovsky and others. A scrutiny of the ballet's native musical ingredients brings the realization that to Stravinsky's compatriots attending the brilliant Diaghilev opening in Paris in 1911, *Petrouchka* offered musical and literary overtones that were lost to the Western listener, presumably ignorant of the folk origin of many of the themes. Yet, in depicting this tragedy of a brow-beaten people, what could be more natural for the composer than to build his thematic material (as in the *Firebird* and *Mavra*) on Russian native songs?

The five songs given here probably do not exhaust the native material in *Petrouchka*[4] but they nevertheless document more fully than has previously been attempted one aspect of an important Stravinsky score. There is, however, no reason to believe that either Stravinsky or his collaborators, Benois and Diaghilev, had any need to consult printed collections of Russian folk songs to draw upon the resources of native tunes, though certain indications point in that direction. In any case, librarians (and musicologists) find it easier to acknowledge the borrowing of folk song material when the models have been located in printed collections.

The first such collection of Russian folk songs *with tunes* was published in 1790 by the Silesian composer Ivan Prach (Johan Gottfried Pratsch). In his second edition of 1806, he noted down a variant of one of the Petrouchka tunes, thus giving documentary evidence that the tune

3. First Picture, [2 measures after 13].
4. Mr. Nikolas Nabokov of St. John's College, Annapolis, informs me that both the main theme of the Russian Dance of the First Picture, particularly as it appears [19 measures after 41], and the gypsy dance in the Fourth Picture, [at 103], are derived from Russian folk songs. Unhappily, Mr. Nabokov cannot recall the texts with which these tunes are associated, and thus far published versions have not been found.

was popular even at this early date. As the nineteenth century wore on dozens of other collections appeared, filled with Russia's rich folk song literature. The bibliography at the end of this article [5] contains eleven collections to which the tunes used in *Petrouchka* have been traced and the notes that follow describe in more detail the character and background of the collections.

To Westerners the familiar names of Tchaikovsky, Balakirev and Rimsky-Korsakov appear to dominate the list. It is a paradox that their fame as composers continues to direct particular attention to their folk song anthologies, although the material presented is actually less authentic than the results of similar studies by such scholars as Melgunov, Istomin and Diutsch, and Lineva. Ambitious composers are sometimes tempted to "improve" on their originals. Tchaikovsky's letter to Balakirev, written from Moscow on December 30, 1868, after Jurgenson had commissioned him to compile a four-hand arrangement of fifty Russian folk songs, leaves little doubt about the liberties he was willing to take.[6]

> "Dearest Mili Alexseyevich:
>
> . . . .
>
> Will you not find it possible to write me two words concerning the following. Jurgenson has ordered from me a four-hand arrangement of fifty Russian songs. Twenty-five of them I have already completed; they are taken from Vilboa's Collection, of course I have buried the Vilboa harmonization and have made my own and have even dared to change in places the very melodies, basing my changes on the general character of the Russian song. Now I would like to take twenty-five songs from your collection and am afraid to cause your displeasure in doing so.
>
> Do let me know: 1) do you want me to preserve your harmonization verbatim and only rearrange it for four hands; * 2) or that this is not at all your wish; 3) or that you would be dissatisfied with me in either case and would not want me to take your songs. In other words, I do not want to do anything before I hear from you.
>
> I take this occasion to send congratulations for the New Year.
>
> P. Tchaikovsky
>
> * In this case the title page would mention of course that the harmonization is yours and has been borrowed by me from you.
>
> P. Tchaikovsky"

5. Omitted in this edition; the details of the particular collections utilized as sources for this article have been transferred to footnotes. [*Editor*]

6. The correspondence between Balakirev and Tchaikovsky was edited by S. Liapunov and published in 1912 under the title "Perepiska M. A. Balakireva s P. I. Chaikovskim, s predisloviem i primiechaniiami S. Liapunova. S. Peterburg, Postavshchik dvora Ego Imperatorskago Velichestva Iulii Genrikh Tsimmerman." The translation of the correspondence given here was kindly supplied by Mrs. Lubov Keefer.

To which Balakirev replied from St. Petersburg on January 15, 1869:

> "My dear Peter Ilyitch:
>   Apologies for long silence. There was much to straighten out after Dargomyjski's death.
>   What concerns my songs, which you desire to arrange for four hands, do with them whatever you prefer. Wherever you may want to leave my harmony intact, do so. Wherever you want to manufacture your own, do it, only do not mention that the songs have been taken from my collection, otherwise I fear that Johanssen will institute a process, I have sold him the publishing rights to my collection.
>   Rimsky-Korsakov sends his greetings. . . .
>
>   M. Balakirev"

When the collection appeared in the following year, twenty-four of Balakirev's forty songs had been arranged for four hands, and of the remaining number twenty-three have been traced to Vilboa models. The search for and eventual acquisition of a reprint of the Jurgenson edition, and the further discovery of another collection of sixty-five songs for voice and piano under the joint editorship of Prokunin and Tchaikovsky, were among the gratifying results of this attempt to identify the native melodies in Stravinsky's ballet, since each of the collections yielded a Petrouchka tune. A third song, with a particularly Stravinskian melodic line, has so far been located only in the collection of Istomin and Diutsch, and for the remaining two songs the most likely sources are two collections of Rimsky-Korsakov, Stravinsky's master.

THE FIVE RUSSIAN FOLK SONGS

The frequent festivals at which the Russian moujik finds release from toil have retained to the present day an intimate blending of pagan and Christian rites. The songs that Stravinsky included in the melodic material of *Petrouchka* range from those sung at Eastertide to those that belong to Midsummer Night, while the ballet itself takes place at Carnival time, known in Russia as *Maslenitza* or Butterweek. Indeed, the juxtaposition of Butterweek, Easter and Midsummer Night may have its significance, for it implies a non-Christian glorification of the growth of new life. Though externally directed by the Church and its feast days, Russian peasant celebrations are fundamentally of a pagan nature, with an emphasis on the months of spring and early summer. The devoutly Christian

Stravinsky himself offered an apotheosis of this in the *Sacre du Printemps,* which represents a pagan rite, sacred to a vernal god of pre-historic Russia. Only at Easter itself is the religious aspect of the festival at the core of the popular celebration.

The Easter song that occurs both in the First and Fourth pictures,[7] though not very widely known, is published in Rimsky-Korsakov's collection of one hundred Russian folk songs. It is called the *Song of the Volochebniki* (from the province of Smolensk) after the singing beggars who wander from village to village at Easter time, felicitating the householders and intoning again and again "For Jesus Christ is arisen." This traditional greeting on Easter Day, given out whenever friends or neighbors meet, brings the response, "He is, indeed, risen," whereupon they embrace, kissing each other on both cheeks.

Song of the Volochebniki [8] (from the Rimsky-Korsakov Collection of 100 Songs [9])

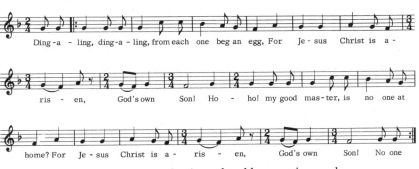

No one comes to the door, the old master is proud,
For Jesus Christ is arisen, God's own Son!

7. [At 2 and 3 in the First Picture, and at 2 measures after 123 in the Fourth Picture.]

8. The translations of all the songs given in this article have been based on prose translations by Mr. Vladimir Gsovski and Mr. George Novossiltzeff of the Library of Congress. The versification of the translations has been somewhat of a community project with the editor of Notes largely responsible. Messrs. Gsovski and Novossiltzeff also supplied numerous details from their knowledge of Russian life, so that in the few places where images have been changed or an idea shifted from one line to another, the basic sense of the passage has been kept. The rich double and triple Russian rhymes could not be reproduced in an undeclined English, but the rhyme schemes, except in the second folksong, have generally been followed even to duplicating shifting patterns and irregularities.

9. *Sbornik russkikh narodnykh piesen sostavlennyĭ Rimskim-Korsakovym,* St. Petersburg, 1877.

> He sits at the table and leans on his cane,
> For Jesus Christ is arisen, God's own Son!
> But if no one will give us a fine chicken pie,
> For Jesus Christ is arisen, God's own Son!
> From him we will take his old cow from the stall,
> For Jesus Christ is arisen, God's own Son!
> And if he will not give us a couple of eggs,
> For Jesus Christ is arisen, God's own Son!
> We'll chase from the meadow his flock of fat sheep,
> For Jesus Christ is arisen, God's own Son!
> If he still will not give us a chunk of corned beef,
> For Jesus Christ is arisen, God's own Son!
> We'll slaughter his pig as he rolls in his sty,
> For Jesus Christ is arisen, God's own Son!

As the celebration of Butterweek reaches a climax in the First Picture, the lively Russian dance of the three puppets takes place. Throughout the first section of the dance can be heard anticipations of the St. John's Eve song [10] until [at number 41] the piano plays a complete version. St. John's Day, the 24th of June, celebrated throughout Europe in all ages, is one of the most popular of the religious festivals and makes good the scriptural prophecy regarding John the Baptist, that "many shall rejoice at his birth." Its importance as a holiday is enhanced because it coincides with Midsummer Day and it has therefore inherited its customs and traditions from heathen times. Festivities begin on St. John's Eve with the lighting of bonfires around which the people dance with almost frantic merriment. This custom has its counterpart in the Johannisfeuer set ablaze in Germany at the time of the June solstice. The magic potions and superstitions of Shakespeare's gossamer tale, the mischievous doings and disturbances of *Johannisnacht* in *Die Meistersinger*, not to speak of Gogol's *Eve of St. John* and Mussorgsky's *Night on the Bare Mountain* (*St. John's Eve*), all acknowledge the generally licentious character of the holiday. Mothers are not expected to exert any control over their daughters, knowing it to be quite useless; indeed, it is the confessions of a maiden's joyous abandon that form the text of our tune.

The editors state that the song was taken down in 1886 in the village of Bashevskaia in the County of Totemsk. It has been found in no other collection, and thus there is reason to suppose that Istomin and Diutsch were the first to publish it when their collection appeared in 1894. Its rarity is such that no Russian to whom it has been shown has recognized

10. [From 2 measures after 34 through the measure before 41.]

Song for St. John's Eve (from the collection of Istomin and Diutsch [11])

I am run-ning, run - ning in_____ the sun - shine_

through the har - vest field_ run - ning I_____ reach a shrine._____

> On the shrine two pigeons sat together,
> One plump pigeon said nothing and did not stir.
>
> But I heard the pigeon on the left say
> That tomorrow will be St. John's holiday.
>
> Then my darling comes to take me with him;
> At the festival we will follow each whim;
>
> Hug and kiss all night with more and more vim.
> At the festival I will tell my young man:
>
> "Don't get married, don't be wed, my young man,
> Don't get married, dare-devil, enjoy your span.
>
> "You will find it nice to play with us girls;
> Life among us maidens continually whirls."

it, and in fact, previous commentators on the folk songs in *Petrouchka* seem not to have realized that this tune, seemingly so typical of Stravinsky, was actually a folk song. Perfect as the tune is for Stravinsky's purpose, its metrical difficulties and crudities possibly limited its diffusion. There is nothing in the original words that could be dignified as a "rhyme scheme." Somehow the weak accentuation of the first line is rhymed with a strong accent at the end of the second. Lines 7–9 rhyme together, but otherwise for the most part the rhymes are imperfect or altogether absent. Since the melody called for an irregular meter within the lines, it was felt that—to save the English translation from utter chaos —it would be better to rhyme some of the couplets in a more regular fashion. The artlessness of the original, however, is doubtless sufficient guarantee that we have here an unadulterated and unpolished product of Russian folk culture, which in turn possibly explains why the song seems to be so little known in Russian cities. In fact, it has been suggested on

11. *Piesni russkago naroda, sobrany v gubeniiakh Arkhangel'skoi ĭ Olonetskoĭ v 1886 godu*, St. Petersburg, 1894.

the grounds of this rarity that possibly Stravinsky picked up the tune in the Istomin and Diutsch collection itself, but of course, until the composer speaks, the idea remains purely conjectural.

Unlike this rare country song for St. John's Eve, the tune of the third is sung widely in Russia to two totally different sets of words. One of these, *Down the Petersky* or *Petersburg Road,* has even been made familiar to Western listeners through the singing and the early Victor recording by the great Russian baritone, Chaliapin.[12] Melgunov prints this version of the song, together with five variant forms of the melody. Rimsky-Korsakov decried the Melgunov settings as barbarous, but modern folk song collectors would be more likely to praise them for their scientific approach. The Rimsky-Korsakov and Tchaikovsky editions are obviously adaptations for rendition by voice and piano or by piano alone. Melgunov reproduces the polyphonic setting inherent in Russian folk songs, with motives wandering through the various parts and with a proper regard for their original texture and flavor as apprehended by him in his field trips. Readers having access to his book may wish to compare his treatment of the song on page 10 of his collection, but since his version is not that used by Stravinsky, and since the apparatus is rather complex, it seems sufficient to give here only the second form of the song.

Known to Russians as "Ia vechor moloda" and possibly more widely spread than the first, it is given in a standardized homophonic setting by both Rimsky-Korsakov and Tchaikovsky. Balakirev used the tune as early as 1858 in his orchestral piece, *Overture on Three Russian Themes.* The form of the melody used by Stravinsky to accompany the Dance of the Nursemaids in the Fourth Picture [13] comes closest to the version given by Rimsky-Korsakov. The structure of the melody calls for short, almost exclamatory phrases of only five syllables, and since this space does not permit of much development of an idea, the poem, even in the original Russian, verges on the impressionistic. Coupled with the difficulty of fitting in sixteen words rhyming with "night," the translators found it necessary to invoke a certain amount of poetic license in dislocating the normal order of the words, but the general psychic crescendo of the young wife—the "moloda" as she reels home may still convey some of the feeling of the original and help to show why it is so popular.

12. Recently reissued on Angel record **COLH** 141 in the series *Great Recordings of the Century.* [*Editor*]

13. [4 measures after 90.]

Dance Song (from the Rimsky-Korsakov Collection of Forty Songs [14])

Ear - li-er to-night, at a— par-ty bright,— At a—par-ty— bright, gos-sip-ing ga-lore,

> Gossiping galore, with the wife next door,
> Mead was not just right, nor was beer my type.
> I drank with delight, vodka so divine,
> Pony not for mine, nor a glass for wine,
> But this young wife might drink a bucket quite,
> Drink a bucket quite, filled to its full height.
> Homeward without fright, through the forest dark,
> 'Cross a field aright, straight upon the mark,
> With the yard in sight, swaying in an arc,
> Grab the gate-post tight, gate-post to me hark,
> "Gate-post, gate-post, mine; you must know my plight,
> Hold me straight in line, tipsy as I am,
> Tipsy as I am, stupid drunken lamb.
> Lord! my husband is such a drunken wight.
> Wine he need not drink, water from the sink.
> Am I not the boss, in this house all right:
> Having scrubbed the porch, with it make some bortch;
> Having cleaned the spoons, bake some pies like moons;
> Keep the house so clean, . . .

The simple love song of a happy bride which continues the music for the Nursemaid's Dance,[15] seemed for a time to defy any satisfactory English rendering because of the conflicting meanings ascribed, both in the literature and by Russian scholars, to the key word of the first three stanzas, here translated by the unpoetic word "doorway." It was obvious from the beginning that the connotations of this Russian love song would be completely misconstrued if its first line, "Akh vy sieni, moi sieni" were incorrectly translated. Tolstoy brings in the singing of the song with fine dramatic effect in *War and Peace,* from which the following excerpt serves to describe its popularity and effect upon the characters in this scene of the novel:

14. *40 narodnykh pesen s soprovozhdeniem fortepiano garmonizovanykh N. Rimskim-Korsakovym,* Moscow, 1919 (reprinted under direction of Filippov from 1882 edition.)

15. [Beginning at 96.]

"Singers to the front!" came the captain's order. And from the different ranks some twenty men ran to the front. A drummer, their leader, turned round facing the singers. . . . Then . . . began:

"Oh, my bower, oh, my bower . . . !

'Oh, my bower new . . . !' chimed in twenty voices. . . . The commander in chief made a sign that the men should continue to march at ease, and he and all his suite showed pleasure at the sound of the singing and the sight of the dancing soldier and gay marching men. The hussar cornet . . . fell back from the carriage and rode up to Dolokhov. The lively song gave a special flavor to the tone of free and easy gaiety with which Zherkov spoke, and to the intentional coldness of Dolokhov's reply.

'She let the hawk fly upward from her wide right sleeve,'

went the song, arousing an involuntary sensation of courage and cheerfulness. Their conversation would probably have been different but for the effect of that song.

'Is it true that Austrians have been beaten?' asked Dolokhov.

'The devil only knows! They say so.'

'I'm glad,' answered Dolokhov briefly and clearly, as the song demanded.

'I say, come round some evening and we'll have a game of faro!' said Zherkov.

'We shall see.'

'It's a long, long way
To my native land . . .'

Zherkov touched his horse with the spurs; . . . galloped past the company and overtook the carriage, still keeping time to the song." [16]

But our Russian translators insisted that while "Oh my bower" was poetically more pleasing it was just as misleading as Roehl's "Ach du mein Häuschen klein" (Oh, my little house) [17] or Johannes von Guenther's "Ach du Kammer, meine Kammer" (Oh, my Chamber) .[18] And as for the only other complete English translation by D. Millar Craig, printed in the Swerkoff collection, this was not only inaccurate but impossible. Craig translates the word as "attic chamber." He was apparently thinking of a princess in her lofty palace, rather than of a peasant's cottage. Literally, "sieni" is the word for the small, unheated entrance room,

16. Leo Tolstoy, *War and Peace*, Tr. by Louise and Aylmer Maude, Simon and Schuster, New York, 1942, pp. 126–127.

17. Tolstoi: *Krieg und Frieden;* Insel Verlag, Leipzig, vol. 1, p. 217.

18. Das Russische Volkslied (ed. Guenther & Westermann) , Munich, Orchis Verlag, a.d.

built on the front of practically every peasant's home and serving as a combination "storm door" to keep the wintry blasts from the main living room on the inside and a vestibule for storing the next few logs destined for the fire. There is no specific word in English which means all of this. "Vestibule" comes closest, but it has three syllables instead of two, so that its frequent introduction proved practically impossible. And yet something in the proximity of the front door was essential, since the song clearly implied that for the young Russian lovers during their courting days the "sieni" offered the same protection as do hallways and doorways all over the world—a refuge between the usual Scylla and Charybdis, the cold outdoors and the family's taunting within. Now that the young woman is married and has her own home with its richly decorated "sieni," carved probably with the typical square patterns, it is no longer necessary to put it to the same purpose, but nonetheless she remembers the little front rooms in her far away native land, where Vaniushka courted her, and therefore has a special fondness for her own.

Akh vy sieni, moi sieni (from the Swerkoff collection [19])

Oh, you door-way, my dear door-way, Oh, my door-way new-ly made, Door-way car-ven from new ma-ple Of a light,[20] pret-ty shade. And if

> And if only I could walk there
> By my doorway late at night
> With my lover holding my hand
> With his own, pressing tight.
>
> A young wife stepped from the entrance,
> From the entrance newly made,
> From the doorway carved from maple
> Of a light, pretty shade.

19. *50 Russian Folk Songs for Voice and Pianoforte,* edited by E. L. Swerkoff, English version by D. Millar Craig, Leipzig, 1937.
20. Swerkoff breaks the regular pulsation by using a quarter note at this point, and the translation was made to fit his version. Stravinsky and most other published versions give four straight eighth notes.

From inside her long right sleeve
Her brave young falcon then she drew,
As the falcon flew away
She told him what he should do.

"Falcon, fly into the sky!
Oh! fly so far and fly so high,
Fly so far and fly so high,
And find my father-in-law.

"Father lives away off there
Where is my own dear native land;
He is very stern and strict
And always rules with firm hand.

"Against wand'ring out at ev'ning
Father placed the strictest ban;
But I paid no heed to father
And amused my young man.

"I amused him for the reason
In his father's eyes he's tops;
And they call him Vaniushka
Who brews beer from green hops."

The tune that accompanies the Dance of the Coachmen and Grooms in the Fourth Picture [21] "*O, snow now thaws,*" (Ulichnaia) is given the heading "Street Song (County of Tombosk)" by its editors. It is a twelve-bar theme which Stravinsky uses in its entirety, breaking it up between different parts of the score. This song is a variant of a more popular tune known as "Umorilas" or by its first line "Ia na gorkku shla." Melodically the song swings along in a stamping rhythm suited to a dance of stable hands. The text offers a lusty picture of lives compounded of fish chowder, noodle soup, and love—an atmosphere, moreover, quite characteristic of the whole group of folk songs on which Stravinsky drew so appositely for the vividest themes of *Petrouchka*.

21. [At 109.]

O! Snow Now Thaws (from the Prokunin-Tchaikovsky collection [22])

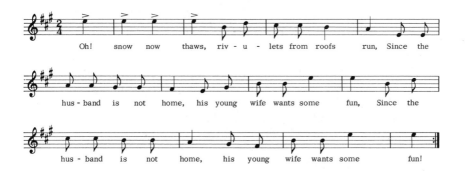

Now rain pours down, reeds on river banks swish,
Neighb'ring lad comes to her door with a fine big white fish.
"Oh neighbor, dear, darling neighbor of mine,
Will you be so kind and cook, a fish chowder so fine.
Fish chowder rich flavored with some parsley tips,
Oh, my neighbor is a dear, just like honey to my lips.
Each day before I had only wheat gruel,
Come to me my darling girl, and my doting heart rule.
Rich noodle soup will to-day be our fare,
Come upon these pillows soft, let us play without care.
All through my life, I shall swig my wine and beer,
And when death comes to my door, I shall go without fear."

22. N. Prokunin, *65 russkikh narodnykh píesen dlía odnogo goloso* s f.p. (P. Chaĭ-kovskiĭ) .

Bibliography

WRITINGS BY STRAVINSKY

Stravinsky, Igor, *Chronicle of My Life,* New York, 1936; *An Autobiography,* New York, 1962 (paperback).

Stravinsky, Igor, *The Diaghilev I Knew,* in *Atlantic Monthly,* CXCII (1953), 33–36.

Stravinsky, Igor, *Poetics of Music in the Form of Six Lessons,* Cambridge, 1947; with preface by Darius Milhaud, New York, 1956 (paperback).

Stravinsky, Igor, and Robert Craft, *Conversations with Igor Stravinsky,* Garden City. N. Y., 1959.

Stravinsky, Igor, and Robert Craft, *Expositions and Developments,* Garden City, N. Y., 1962.

Stravinsky, Igor, and Robert Craft, *Memories and Commentaries,* Garden City, N. Y., 1960.

GENERAL LITERATURE ON STRAVINSKY

Berger, Arthur, *Music for the Ballet,* in *Dance Index,* VI (1947), 258–77.

Blitzstein, Marc, *The Phenomenon of Stravinsky,* in *The Musical Quarterly,* XXI (1935), 330–47.

Boys, Henry, *Stravinsky: The Musical Materials,* in *The Score,* 4 (1951), 11–18.

Calvocoressi, M. D., *A Russian Composer of To-day,* in *Musical Times,* LII (1911), 511–12.
This is the first mention of Stravinsky in English.

Cazden, Norman, *Humor in the Music of Stravinsky and Prokofiev,* in *Science and Society,* XVIII (1954), 52–74.

Collaer, Paul, *Strawinsky,* Brussels, 1930.

Hill, Edward B., *A Note on Stravinsky,* in *Harvard Musical Review,* II/7 (1914), 3–7, 23.
Probably the first critical mention of Stravinsky in America.

Kall, Alexis, *Stravinsky in the Chair of Poetry,* in *The Musical Quarterly,* XXVI (1940), 283–96.

Keller, Hans, *Rhythm: Gershwin and Stravinsky,* in *The Score,* 20 (1957), 19–31.

Lang, Paul Henry, ed., *Stravinsky: A New Appraisal of His Work,* New York, 1963 (paperback).

Lederman, Minna, *Stravinsky in the Theatre*, New York, 1949.
  Contains (pp. 191–228) a bibliography.
Murrill, H., *Aspects of Stravinsky*, in *Music & Letters*, XXXII (1951), 118–24.
Schaeffner, André, *Strawinsky*, Paris, 1931.
Stravinsky, Igor: A Complete Catalogue of His Published Works, London, 1957;
  rev. ed., 1962.
Tansman, Alexandre, *Igor Stravinsky: The Man and His Music*, New York,
  1949.
Vlad, Roman, *Stravinsky*, New York, 1960.
White, Eric Walter, *Stravinsky: A Critical Survey*, London, 1947.
White, Eric Walter, *Stravinsky: The Composer and His Music*, Berkeley, 1966.
Wise, C. Stanley, *Impressions of Igor Stravinsky*, in *Musical Quarterly*, II (1916),
  249–56.

SPECIFIC LITERATURE ON *Petrushka*

Benois, Alexandre, *Reminiscences of the Russian Ballet*, London, 1941.
  Chapter VIII of Part Three (pp. 323–38) devoted to *Petrushka*.
Boys, Henry, *Note on the New Petrouchka*, in *Tempo*, Summer 1948, pp. 15–18.
Cocteau, Jean, *Igor Stravinsky und das russische Ballett*, in *Melos*, XV (1948),
  268–71.
Drew, David, *Stravinsky's Revisions*, in *The Score*, 20 (June 1957), 47–57.
Evans, Edwin, *Stravinsky: The Fire-Bird and Petrushka*, London, 1933.
Fokine, Michel, *Memoirs of a Ballet Master*, Boston, 1961.
  Chapter X (pp. 183–94) on *Petrushka*.
Grigoriev, S. L., *The Diaghilev Ballet 1909–1929*, London, 1953; also in
  Penguin paperback, 1960.
Lawrence, Robert, *Petrouchka; A Ballet*, New York, 1940.
Lieven, Prince Peter, *The Birth of Ballets-Russes*, London, 1936.
  Chapter VIII (pp. 130–53) on *Petrushka*.
Magriel, Paul, ed., *Nijinsky: An Illustrated Monograph*, New York, 1946.
Nijinsky, Romola, *Nijinsky*, New York, 1936.
Schmidt-Garre, Helmut, *Die Fokin-Ära des Diaghilew Balletts*, in *Neue
  Zeitschrift für Musik*, CXXVI (March 3, 1965), 96–98.
Stephan, Rudolf, *Vom alten und vom neuen Petrushka*, in *Neue Zeitschrift
  für Musik*, 123 (June 1962), 255–61.
Van Vechten, Carl, *Music After the Great War and Other Studies*, 2nd ed.,
  New York, 1915.

Charles Hamm, a professor of musicology at the University of Illinois, has published books on the music of Guillaume Dufay and opera, and has contributed articles and reviews on music of the Renaissance, notation, American music, opera, and contemporary music to leading journals in this country and Europe. He holds a doctorate from Princeton University, and was awarded both a Guggenheim Fellowship and a research grant from the Fulbright Commission for study in Italy for the year 1967–68. He is editing the works of Leonel Power for the American Institute of Musicology.